Microsoft Office 2010
Keyboard Shortcuts

For Windows

Compiled By

U. C-Abel Books.

All Rights Reserved

First Edition: 2016

Copyright @ U. C-Abel Books. ISBN 13: 978-978-54574-2-1.

ISBN 13: 978-978-54574-2-1.
ISBN-10: 9785457427

Published by U. C-Abel Books.

A Summarized Table Of Contents.

Table of Contents

Acknowledgement.

U. C-Abel Books will not take all the credits for Microsoft Office 2010 keyboard shortcuts listed in this book, but shares it with Microsoft Corporation as some of the shortcut keys came from them and are "used with permission from Microsoft".

Dedication

This book is dedicated to computer users and lovers of keyboard shortcuts all over the world.

Introduction.

We enjoy using shortcut keys because they set us on a high plane that astonishes people around us when we work with them. As wonderful shortcuts users, the worst eyesore we witness in computing is to see somebody sluggishly struggling to execute a task through mouse usage when in actual sense shortcuts will help save that person the overall time. Most people have asked us to help them with a list of shortcut keys that can make them work as smartly as we do and that drove us into research to broaden our knowledge and truly help them as they demanded, that is the reason for the existence of this book. It is a great tool for lovers of shortcuts, and those who want to join the group.

Most times, the things we love don't come by easily. It is our love for keyboard shortcuts that made us to bear long sleepless nights like owls, just to make sure we get the best out of it, and it is the best we got that we are sharing with you in this book. You cannot be the same at computing after reading this book. The time you entrusted to our care is an expensive possession and we promise not to mess it up.

Thank you.

What to Know Before You Begin.

General Notes.

1. It is important to note that when using shortcuts to perform any command, you should make sure the target area is active, if not, you may get a wrong result. Example, if you want to highlight all texts, you must make sure the text field is active and if an object, make sure the object area is active. The active area is always known by the location where the cursor of your computer blinks.

2. Most of the keyboard shortcuts you will see in this book refer to the U.S. keyboard layout. Keys for other layouts might not correspond exactly to the keys on a U.S. keyboard.

3. The plus (+) signs that come in the middle of keyboard shortcuts simply mean the keys are meant to be combined or held down together not to be added as one of the shortcut keys. In a case where plus sign is needed; it will be duplicated (++).

4. For keyboard shortcuts in which you press one key immediately followed by another key, the keys are separated by a comma (,).

5. It is also important to note that the shortcut keys listed in this book are for Microsoft Office 2010.

Microsoft Excel 2010.

If you are using Microsoft Excel Starter 2010, be aware that not all the features listed for Excel are supported in Excel Starter 2010.

Microsoft Word 2010.

If you are using Microsoft Word Starter, be aware that not all the features listed for Word are supported in Word Starter.

Microsoft Outlook 2010

Some of the contents of this topic may not be applicable to some languages.

Microsoft OneNote 2010.

Some of the content in this chapter may not be applicable to some languages.

Microsoft SharePoint Server 2010.

Keyboard shortcuts are designed to work with supported Web browsers. The behavior of keyboard shortcuts differs depending on the browser that you use. For example, in Windows Internet Explorer, the shortcut key combination that is assigned to a hyperlink places the active focus on that hyperlink. You must then press ENTER to follow the hyperlink. In Firefox, pressing the key combination follows the link automatically.

In browsers that do not support shortcut key combinations, you may still be able to use the TAB key to move between commands.

If your organization upgraded from a previous version of SharePoint, the server administrator had the option to postpone the application of the user interface (UI) changes, which include the ribbon. This may have been done as a short-term strategy to help ensure that highly customized pages still function with the new SharePoint 2010 UI.

Short Forms Used in This Book and Their Full Meaning.

The following are short forms of keyboard shortcuts used in this Microsoft Office 2010 Keyboard Shortcuts book and their full meaning.

1. Alt - Alternate Key
2. F - Function Key
3. Ctrl - Control Key
4. Shft - Shift Key
5. Win - Windows logo key
6. Tab - Tabulate Key
7. Num Lock - Number Lock Key
8. Esc - Escape Key
9. Caps Lock - Caps Lock Key

CHAPTER 1

Gathering The Basic Knowledge Of Keyboard Shortcuts.

Without the existence of the keyboard, there wouldn't have been anything like keyboard shortcuts, so in this chapter we will learn a little about keyboard before moving to keyboard shortcuts.

1. The Operating Modes Of The Keyboard.

Just like the mouse the keyboard has two operating modes. The two modes are Text Entering and Command Mode.

a. **Text Entering Mode:** this mode gives the operator/user the opportunity to type text.

b. **Command Mode:** this is used to command the operating system/software/application to execute commands in certain ways.

2. Ways To Improve In Your Typing Skill.

1. Put Your Eyes Off The Keyboard.

This is the aspect of keyboard usage that many don't find funny because they always ask. "How can I put my eyes off the keyboard when I am running away from the occurrence of errors on my file?" My aim is to be fast, is this not going to slow me down?

Of course, there will be errors and at the same time your speed will slow down but the motive behind the introduction of this method is to make you faster than you are. Looking at your keyboard while you type can make you get a sore neck, it is better you learn to touch type because the more you type with your eyes fixed on the screen instead of the keyboard, the faster you become.

An alternative to keeping your eyes off your keyboard is to use the "*Das Keyboard Ultimate*".

2. Errors Challenge You

It is better to fail than not to try at all. Not trying at all is an attribute of the weak and lazybones. When you make mistakes, try again because errors are opportunities for improvement.

3. Good Posture (Position Yourself Well).

Do not adopt an awkward position while typing. You should get everything on your desk organized or arranged before sitting to type. Your posture while typing contributes to your speed and productivity.

4. Practice

Here is the conclusion of everything said above. You have to practice your shortcuts constantly. The practice alone is a way of improvement. "Practice brings improvement". Practice always.

3. Software That Will Help You Improve In Your Typing Skill.

There are several Software programs for typing that both kids and adults can use for their typing skill. Here is a list of software that can help you improve in your typing: Mavis Beacon, Typing Instructor, Mucky Typing Adventure, Rapid Tying Tutor, Letter Chase Tying Tutor, Alice Touch Typing Tutor and many more. Personally, I recommend Mavis Beacon.

To learn typing with MAVIS BEACON, install Mavis Beacon software to your computer, start with keyboard lesson, then move to games. Games like ***Penguin Crossing, Creature Lab*** or ***Space Junk*** will help you become a professional in typing. Typing and shortcuts work hand-in-hand.

4. Definition Of Keyboard Shortcuts.

Keyboard shortcuts are defined as a series of keys, sometimes with combination that execute tasks that typically involve the use of mouse or other input devices.

5. Why You Should Shortcut.

1. One may not be able to use a computer mouse easily because of disability or pain.

2. One may not be able to see the mouse pointer as a result of vision impairment, in such case what will the person do? The answer is SHORTCUT.

3. Research has made it known that Extensive mouse usage is related to Repetitive Syndrome Injury (RSI) greatly than the use of keyboard.

4. Keyboard shortcuts speed up computer users, making learning them a worthwhile effort.

5. When performing a job that requires precision, it is wise that you use the keyboard instead of mouse, for instance, if you are dealing with Text Editing, it is better you handle it through keyboard shortcuts than spending more time with mouse alone.

6. Studies calculate that using keyboard shortcuts allows working 10 times faster than working with the mouse. The time you spend looking for the mouse and then getting the cursor to the position you want is lost! Reducing your work duration by 10 times brings you greater results.

6. Ways To Become A Lover Of Shortcuts.

1. Always have the urge to learn new shortcut keys associated with the programs you use.
2. Be happy whenever you learn a new shortcut.
3. Try as much as you can to apply the new shortcuts you learnt.
4. Always bear it in mind that learning new shortcuts is worth it.
5. Always remember that the use of keyboard shortcuts keeps people healthy while performing computing activities.

7. How To Learn New Shortcut Keys

1. Do a research for them: quick reference (a cheat sheet comprehensively arranged) can go a long way to help you improve.
2. Buy applications that show you keyboard shortcuts every time you execute an action with the mouse.
3. Disconnect your mouse if you must learn this fast.
4. Reading user manuals and help topics (Whether offline or online).

8. Your Reward For Knowing Shortcut Keys.

1. You will get faster unimaginably.
2. Your level of efficiency will increase.
3. You will find it easy to use.
4. Opportunities are high that you will become an expert in what you do.
5. You won't have to go for **Office button**, click **New, **click **Blank and Recent** and click **Create** just to insert a fresh/blank page. **Ctrl +N** takes care of that in a second.

A Funny Note: Keyboard shortcuts and Mousing are in a marital union with the use of keyboard shortcuts being the head of the family and it will be very bad for anybody to put asunder between them.

9. Why We Emphasize On The Use of Shortcuts.

You may never ditch your mouse completely unless you are ready to make your brain a box of keyboard shortcuts which will really be frustrating. Just imagine yourself learning all the shortcuts for the program you use and its various versions. You shouldn't learn keyboard shortcuts like that.

Why we are emphasizing on the use of shortcuts is because mouse usage is becoming unusually common and unhealthy, too. So we just want to make sure both are combined so you can get fast, productive and healthy in your computing activities. All you need to know is just the most useful ones of the programs you use.

CHAPTER 2

Keyboard Shortcuts In Excel 2010.

Definition of Program: Microsoft Excel is an electronic spreadsheet program that enables its users to create, organize, format, and calculate data. It was first released for Macintosh in the year 1985 and later on released for Windows in 1987.

Keyboard Access To The Ribbon.

If you're new to the ribbon, the information in this section can help you understand the ribbon's keyboard shortcut model. The ribbon comes with new shortcuts, called **Key Tips**. To make the Key Tips appear, press ALT.

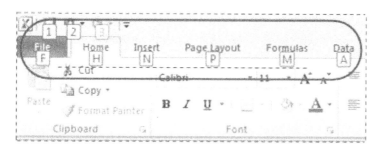

To display a tab on the ribbon, press the key for the tab— for example, press the letter N for the **Insert** tab or M for the **Formulas** tab. This makes all the Key Tip badges for that tab's buttons appear. Then, press the key for the button you want.

Will my old shortcuts still work?

Keyboard shortcuts that begin with CTRL will still work in Excel 2010. For example, CTRL+C still copies to the clipboard, and CTRL+V still pastes from the clipboard.

Most of the old ALT+ menu shortcuts still work, too. However, you need to know the full shortcut from memory — there are no screen reminders of what letters to press. For example, try pressing ALT, and then press one of the old menu keys E (Edit), V (View), I (Insert), and so on. A box pops up saying you're using an access key from an earlier version of Microsoft Office. If you know the entire key sequence, go ahead and initiate the command. If you don't know the sequence, press ESC and use Key Tip badges instead.

The following keyboard shortcuts will help you become a successful user of Microsoft Excel 2010.

CTRL Combination Shortcut Keys.

SHORTCUT	TASK
CTRL+PgUp	Switches between worksheet tabs, from left-to-right.
CTRL+PgDn	Switches between worksheet tabs, from right-to-left.
CTRL+SHIFT+(	Unhides any hidden rows within the selection.
CTRL+SHIFT+&	Applies the outline border to the selected cells.
CTRL+SHIFT_	Removes the outline border from the selected cells.

CTRL+SHIFT+~	Applies the General number format.
CTRL+SHIFT+$	Applies the Currency format with two decimal places (negative numbers in parentheses).
CTRL+SHIFT+%	Applies the Percentage format with no decimal places.
CTRL+SHIFT+^	Applies the Scientific number format with two decimal places.
CTRL+SHIFT+#	Applies the Date format with the day, month, and year.
CTRL+SHIFT+@	Applies the Time format with the hour and minute, and AM or PM.
CTRL+SHIFT+!	Applies the Number format with two decimal places, thousands separator, and minus sign (-) for negative values.
CTRL+SHIFT+*	Selects the current region around the active cell (the data area enclosed by blank rows and blank columns). In a PivotTable, it selects the entire PivotTable report.
CTRL+SHIFT+:	Enters the current time.
CTRL+SHIFT+"	Copies the value from the cell above the active cell into the cell or the Formula Bar.
CTRL+SHIFT+Plus (+)	Displays the **Insert** dialog box to insert blank cells.
CTRL+Minus (-)	Displays the **Delete** dialog box to delete the selected cells.
CTRL+;	Enters the current date.

CTRL+`	Alternates between displaying cell values and displaying formulas in the worksheet.
CTRL+'	Copies a formula from the cell above the active cell into the cell or the Formula Bar.
CTRL+1	Displays the **Format Cells** dialog box.
CTRL+2	Applies or removes bold formatting.
CTRL+3	Applies or removes italic formatting.
CTRL+4	Applies or removes underlining.
CTRL+5	Applies or removes strikethrough.
CTRL+6	Alternates between hiding and displaying objects.
CTRL+8	Displays or hides the outline symbols.
CTRL+9	Hides the selected rows.
CTRL+0	Hides the selected columns.
CTRL+A	Selects the entire worksheet. If the worksheet contains data, CTRL+A selects the current region. Pressing CTRL+A a second time selects the entire worksheet. When the insertion point is to the right of a function name in a formula, displays the **Function Arguments** dialog box. CTRL+SHIFT+A inserts the argument names and parentheses when the insertion point is to the

	right of a function name in a formula.
CTRL+B	Applies or removes bold formatting.
CTRL+C	Copies the selected cells.
CTRL+D	Uses the **Fill Down** command to copy the contents and format of the topmost cell of a selected range into the cells below.
CTRL+F	Displays the **Find and Replace** dialog box, with the **Find** tab selected. SHIFT+F5 also displays this tab, while SHIFT+F4 repeats the last **Find** action. CTRL+SHIFT+F opens the **Format Cells** dialog box with the **Font** tab selected.
CTRL+G	Displays the **Go To** dialog box. F5 also displays this dialog box.
CTRL+H	Displays the **Find and Replace** dialog box, with the **Replace** tab selected.
CTRL+I	Applies or removes italic formatting.
CTRL+K	Displays the **Insert Hyperlink** dialog box for new hyperlinks or the **Edit Hyperlink** dialog box for selected existing hyperlinks.
CTRL+L	Displays the **Create Table** dialog box.
CTRL+N	Creates a new, blank workbook.

CTRL+O	Displays the **Open** dialog box to open or find a file. CTRL+SHIFT+O selects all cells that contain comments.
CTRL+P	Displays the **Print** tab in Microsoft Office Backstage view. CTRL+SHIFT+P opens the **Format Cells** dialog box with the **Font** tab selected.
CTRL+R	Uses the **Fill Right** command to copy the contents and format of the leftmost cell of a selected range into the cells to the right.
CTRL+S	Saves the active file with its current file name, location, and file format.
CTRL+T	Displays the **Create Table** dialog box.
CTRL+U	Applies or removes underlining. CTRL+SHIFT+U switches between expanding and collapsing of the formula bar.
CTRL+V	Inserts the contents of the Clipboard at the insertion point and replaces any selection. Available only after you have cut or copied an object, text, or cell contents. CTRL+ALT+V displays the **Paste Special** dialog box. Available only after you have cut or copied an

	object, text, or cell contents on a worksheet or in another program.
CTRL+W	Closes the selected workbook window.
CTRL+X	Cuts the selected cells.
CTRL+Y	Repeats the last command or action, if possible.
CTRL+Z	Uses the **Undo** command to reverse the last command or to delete the last entry that you typed.

Tip: The CTRL combinations CTRL+E, CTRL+J, CTRL+M, and CTRL+Q are currently unassigned shortcuts.

Function Keys.

SHORTCUT	TASK
F1	Displays the **Excel Help** task pane. CTRL+F1 displays or hides the ribbon. ALT+F1 creates an embedded chart of the data in the current range. ALT+SHIFT+F1 inserts a new worksheet.
F2	Edits the active cell and positions the insertion point at the end of the cell contents. It also moves the insertion point into the Formula Bar when editing in a cell is turned off.

	SHIFT+F2 adds or edits a cell comment. CTRL+F2 displays the print preview area on the **Print** tab in the Backstage view.
F3	Displays the **Paste Name** dialog box. Available only if there are existing names in the workbook. SHIFT+F3 displays the **Insert Function** dialog box.
F4	Repeats the last command or action, if possible. When a cell reference or range is selected in a formula, F4 cycles through all the various combinations of absolute and relative references. CTRL+F4 closes the selected workbook window. ALT+F4 closes Excel.
F5	Displays the **Go To** dialog box. CTRL+F5 restores the window size of the selected workbook window.
F6	Switches between the worksheet, ribbon, task pane, and Zoom controls. In a worksheet that has been split (**View** menu, **Manage This Window**, **Freeze Panes**, **Split Window** command), F6 includes the split panes when switching between panes and the ribbon area.

	SHIFT+F6 switches between the worksheet, Zoom controls, task pane, and ribbon. CTRL+F6 switches to the next workbook window when more than one workbook window is open.
F7	Displays the **Spelling** dialog box to check spelling in the active worksheet or selected range. CTRL+F7 performs the **Move** command on the workbook window when it is not maximized. Use the arrow keys to move the window, and when finished press ENTER, or ESC to cancel.
F8	Turns extend mode on or off. In extend mode, **Extended Selection** appears in the status line, and the arrow keys extend the selection. SHIFT+F8 enables you to add a nonadjacent cell or range to a selection of cells by using the arrow keys. CTRL+F8 performs the **Size** command (on the **Control** menu for the workbook window) when a workbook is not maximized. ALT+F8 displays the **Macro** dialog box to create, run, edit, or delete a macro.
F9	Calculates all worksheets in all open workbooks.

	SHIFT+F9 calculates the active worksheet. CTRL+ALT+F9 calculates all worksheets in all open workbooks, regardless of whether they have changed since the last calculation. CTRL+ALT+SHIFT+F9 rechecks dependent formulas, and then calculates all cells in all open workbooks, including cells not marked as needing to be calculated. CTRL+F9 minimizes a workbook window to an icon.
F10	Turns key tips on or off. (Pressing ALT does the same thing.) SHIFT+F10 displays the shortcut menu for a selected item. ALT+SHIFT+F10 displays the menu or message for an Error Checking button. CTRL+F10 maximizes or restores the selected workbook window.
F11	Creates a chart of the data in the current range in a separate Chart sheet. SHIFT+F11 inserts a new worksheet. ALT+F11 opens the Microsoft Visual Basic For Applications Editor, in which

	you can create a macro by using Visual Basic for Applications (VBA).
F12	Displays the **Save As** dialog box.

Insert A SmartArt Graphic In An Office Document.

1. In the Microsoft Office program where you want to insert the graphic, press Alt, then N, and then M to open the **SmartArt Graphic** dialog box.
2. Press Up Arrow or Down Arrow to select the type of graphic that you want.
3. Press Tab to move to the Layout task pane.
4. Press the arrow keys to select the layout that you want.
5. Press Enter to insert the selected layout.

Work With Shapes In A SmartArt Graphic.

TASK	SHORTCUT
Select the next element in a SmartArt graphic.	Tab
Select the previous element in a SmartArt graphic.	Shift+Tab
Select all shapes.	Ctrl +A
Remove focus from the selected shape.	Esc
Nudge the selected shape up.	Up Arrow
Nudge the selected shape down.	Down Arrow
Nudge the selected shape left.	Left Arrow
Nudge the selected shape right.	Right Arrow
Edit text in the selected shape.	Enter or F2, Esc to exit shape
Delete the selected shape.	Delete or Backspace

Cut the selected shape.	Ctrl+X or Shift+Delete
Copy the selected shape.	Ctrl+C
Paste the contents of the Clipboard.	Ctrl+V
Undo the last action.	Ctrl+Z

Move And Resize Shapes In A Smartart Graphic

TASK	SHORTCUT
Enlarge the selected shape horizontally.	Shift+Right Arrow
Reduce the selected shape horizontally.	Shift+Left Arrow
Enlarge the selected shape vertically.	Shift+Up Arrow
Reduce the selected shape vertically.	Shift+Down Arrow
Rotate the selected shape to the right.	Alt+Right Arrow
Rotate the selected shape to the left.	Alt+Left Arrow

Notes:

- To apply more precise adjustments to shapes, press the Ctrl key in addition to any of the above keyboard shortcuts.
- These keyboard shortcuts apply to multiple selections as if you selected each item individually.

Work With Text In A SmartArt Graphic.

TASK	SHORTCUT
Move one character to the left.	Left Arrow
Move one character to the right.	Right Arrow
Move up one line.	Up Arrow
Move down one line.	Down Arrow
Move one word to the left.	Ctrl+Left Arrow
Move one word to the right.	Ctrl+Right Arrow
Move one paragraph up.	Ctrl+Up Arrow
Move one paragraph down.	Ctrl+Down Arrow
Move to the end of a line.	End
Move to the beginning of a line.	Home
Move to the end of a text box.	Ctrl+End
Move to the beginning of a text box.	Ctrl+Home
Cut selected text.	Ctrl+X
Copy selected text.	Ctrl+C
Paste selected text.	Ctrl+V
Move the selected text up.	Alt+Shift+Up Arrow
Move the selected text down.	Alt+Shift+Down Arrow
Undo the last action.	Ctrl+Z
Delete one character to the left.	Backspace
Delete one word to the left.	Ctrl+Backspace
Delete one character to the right.	Delete
Delete one word to the right.	Ctrl+Delete
Promote the selected text.	Alt+Shift+Left Arrow
Demote the selected text.	Alt+Shift+Right Arrow
Check the spelling (not available in Word).	F7

Apply Character Formatting

TASK	SHORTCUT
Open the **Font** dialog box.	Ctrl+Shift+F or Ctrl+Shift+P
Increase the font size of the selected text.	Ctrl+Shift+>
Decrease the font size of the selected text.	Ctrl+Shift+<
Switch the case of selected text (lower case, Title Case, UPPER CASE).	Shift+F3
Apply bold formatting to the selected text.	Ctrl+B
Apply an underline to the selected text.	Ctrl+U
Apply italic formatting to the selected text.	Ctrl+I
Apply subscript formatting to the selected text.	Ctrl+Equal Sign
Apply superscript formatting to the selected text.	Ctrl+Shift+Plus Sign
Adjust the superscript/subscript offset up.	Ctrl+Alt+Shift+>
Adjust the superscript/subscript offset down.	Ctrl+Alt+Shift+<
Remove all character formatting from the selected text.	Shift+Ctrl+Spacebar

Copy Text Formatting

TASK	SHORTCUT
Copy formatting from the selected text.	Shift+Ctrl+C
Paste formatting to the selected text.	Shift+Ctrl+V

Apply Paragraph Formatting

TASK	SHORTCUT
Center a paragraph.	Ctrl+E
Justify a paragraph.	Ctrl+J
Left align a paragraph.	Ctrl+L
Right align a paragraph.	Ctrl+R
Demote a bullet point.	Tab or Alt+Shift+Right Arrow
Promote a bullet point.	Shift+Tab or Alt+Shift+Left Arrow

Use The Text Pane

TASK	SHORTCUT
Merge two lines of text.	Delete at the end of the first line of text
Display the shortcut menu.	Shift+F10
Switch between the **Text** pane and the drawing canvas.	Ctrl+Shift+F2
Close the **Text** pane.	Alt+F4
Switch the focus from the **Text** pane to the border of the SmartArt graphic.	Esc
Open the SmartArt graphics Help topic. (Your pointer should be in the Text pane.)	Ctrl +Shift+F1

Other Useful Shortcut Keys

SHORTCUT	TASK
ALT	Displays the Key Tips (new shortcuts) on the ribbon.
	For example,
	ALT, W, P switches the worksheet to Page Layout view.
	ALT, W, L switches the worksheet to Normal view.
	ALT, W, I switches the worksheet to Page Break Preview view.
ARROW KEYS	Move one cell up, down, left, or right in a worksheet.
	CTRL+ARROW KEY moves to the edge of the current data region in a worksheet.
	SHIFT+ARROW KEY extends the selection of cells by one cell.
	CTRL+SHIFT+ARROW KEY extends the selection of cells to the last nonblank cell in the same column or row as the active cell, or if the next cell is blank, extends the selection to the next nonblank cell.
	LEFT ARROW or RIGHT ARROW selects the tab to the left or right when the ribbon is selected. When a submenu

	is open or selected, these arrow keys switch between the main menu and the submenu. When a ribbon tab is selected, these keys navigate the tab buttons. DOWN ARROW or UP ARROW selects the next or previous command when a menu or submenu is open. When a ribbon tab is selected, these keys navigate up or down the tab group. In a dialog box, arrow keys move between options in an open drop-down list, or between options in a group of options. DOWN ARROW or ALT+DOWN ARROW opens a selected drop-down list.
BACKSPACE	Deletes one character to the left in the Formula Bar. Also clears the content of the active cell. In cell editing mode, it deletes the character to the left of the insertion point.
DELETE	Removes the cell contents (data and formulas) from selected cells without affecting cell formats or comments. In cell editing mode, it deletes the character to the right of the insertion point.

END	END turns End mode on. In End mode, you can then press an arrow key to move to the next nonblank cell in the same column or row as the active cell. If the cells are blank, pressing END followed by an arrow key moves to the last cell in the row or column.
	END also selects the last command on the menu when a menu or submenu is visible.
	CTRL+END moves to the last cell on a worksheet, to the lowest used row of the rightmost used column. If the cursor is in the formula bar, CTRL+END moves the cursor to the end of the text.
	CTRL+SHIFT+END extends the selection of cells to the last used cell on the worksheet (lower-right corner). If the cursor is in the formula bar, CTRL+SHIFT+END selects all text in the formula bar from the cursor position to the end—this does not affect the height of the formula bar.
ENTER	Completes a cell entry from the cell or the Formula Bar, and selects the cell below (by default).
	In a data form, it moves to the first field in the next record.

	Opens a selected menu (press F10 to activate the menu bar) or performs the action for a selected command. In a dialog box, it performs the action for the default command button in the dialog box (the button with the bold outline, often the **OK** button). ALT+ENTER starts a new line in the same cell. CTRL+ENTER fills the selected cell range with the current entry. SHIFT+ENTER completes a cell entry and selects the cell above.
ESC	Cancels an entry in the cell or Formula Bar. Closes an open menu or submenu, dialog box, or message window. It also closes full screen mode when this mode has been applied, and returns to normal screen mode to display the ribbon and status bar again.
HOME	Moves to the beginning of a row in a worksheet. Moves to the cell in the upper-left corner of the window when SCROLL LOCK is turned on.

	Selects the first command on the menu when a menu or submenu is visible. CTRL+HOME moves to the beginning of a worksheet. CTRL+SHIFT+HOME extends the selection of cells to the beginning of the worksheet.
PAGE DOWN	Moves one screen down in a worksheet. ALT+PAGE DOWN moves one screen to the right in a worksheet. CTRL+PAGE DOWN moves to the next sheet in a workbook. CTRL+SHIFT+PAGE DOWN selects the current and next sheet in a workbook.
PAGE UP	Moves one screen up in a worksheet. ALT+PAGE UP moves one screen to the left in a worksheet. CTRL+PAGE UP moves to the previous sheet in a workbook. CTRL+SHIFT+PAGE UP selects the current and previous sheet in a workbook.
SPACEBAR	In a dialog box, performs the action for the selected button, or selects or clears a check box.

	CTRL+SPACEBAR selects an entire column in a worksheet. SHIFT+SPACEBAR selects an entire row in a worksheet. CTRL+SHIFT+SPACEBAR selects the entire worksheet. • If the worksheet contains data, CTRL+SHIFT+SPACEBAR selects the current region. Pressing CTRL+SHIFT+SPACEBAR a second time selects the current region and its summary rows. Pressing CTRL+SHIFT+SPACEBAR a third time selects the entire worksheet. • When an object is selected, CTRL+SHIFT+SPACEBAR selects all objects on a worksheet. ALT+SPACEBAR displays the **Control** menu for the Excel window.
TAB	Moves one cell to the right in a worksheet. Moves between unlocked cells in a protected worksheet. Moves to the next option or option group in a dialog box.

	SHIFT+TAB moves to the previous cell in a worksheet or the previous option in a dialog box.
	CTRL+TAB switches to the next tab in dialog box.
	CTRL+SHIFT+TAB switches to the previous tab in a dialog box.

Use the keyboard to work with the ribbon

Do tasks quickly without using the mouse by pressing a few keys—no matter where you are in an Office program. You can get to every command on the ribbon by using an access key—usually by pressing two to four keys.

1. Press and release the ALT key.
2. You see the little boxes called KeyTips over each command available in the current view.
3. Press the letter shown in the KeyTip over the command you want to use.
4. Depending on which letter you pressed, you might see additional KeyTips. For example, if the **Home** tab is active and you pressed N, the **Insert** tab is displayed, along with the KeyTips for the groups in that tab.
5. Continue pressing letters until you press the letter of the specific command you want to use.

Tip: To cancel the action you're taking and hide the KeyTips, press and release the ALT key.

Change the keyboard focus without using the mouse

Another way to use the keyboard to work with the ribbon is to move the focus among the tabs and commands until you find the feature you want to use. The following shows some ways to move the keyboard focus without using the mouse.

TASK	SHORTCUT
Select the active tab and show the access keys.	ALT or F10. Press either of these keys again to move back to the Office file and cancel the access keys.
Move to another tab.	ALT or F10 to select the active tab, and then LEFT ARROW or RIGHT ARROW.
Move to another Group on the active tab.	ALT or F10 to select the active tab, and then CTRL+RIGHT ARROW or LEFT ARROW to move between groups.
Minimize (collapse) or restore the ribbon.	CTRL+F1
Display the shortcut menu for the selected item.	SHIFT+F10
Move the focus to select the active tab, your Office file, task pane, or status bar.	F6
Move the focus to each command in the ribbon, forward or backward.	ALT or F10, and then TAB or SHIFT+TAB
Move down, up, left, or right among the items in the ribbon.	DOWN ARROW, UP ARROW, LEFT ARROW, or RIGHT ARROW

Go to the selected command or control in the ribbon.	SPACE BAR or ENTER
Open the selected menu or gallery in the ribbon.	SPACE BAR or ENTER
Go to a command or option in the ribbon so you can change it.	ENTER
Finish changing the value of a command or option in the ribbon, and move focus back to the Office file.	ENTER
Get help on the selected command or control in the ribbon. (If no Help article is associated with the selected command, the Help table of contents for that program is shown instead.)	F1

Note: If you are using Microsoft Excel Starter 2010, be aware that not all the features listed for Excel are supported in Excel Starter 2010.

CHAPTER 3

Keyboard Shortcuts In PowerPoint 2010.

Definition of Program: Microsoft PowerPoint is a Microsoft Corporation program designed in 1990 used for graphic presentation.

The following keyboard shortcuts will help you become a successful user of Microsoft PowerPoint 2010.

Keyboard Shortcuts To Use When Creating A Presentation.

Online Help

Keyboard shortcuts for use in the Help window

The Help window provides access to all Office Help content. The Help window displays topics and other Help content.

In The Help Window

TASK	SHORTCUT
Open the Help window.	F1
Close the Help window.	ALT+F4
Switch between the Help window and the active program.	ALT+TAB

Go back to **PowerPoint** Help and How-to table of contents.	ALT+HOME
Select the next item in the Help window.	TAB
Select the previous item in the Help window.	SHIFT+TAB
Perform the action for the selected item.	ENTER
In the **Browse PowerPoint Help** section of the Help window, select the next or previous item, respectively.	TAB, SHIFT+TAB
In the **Browse PowerPoint Help** section of the Help window, expand or collapse the selected item, respectively.	ENTER
Select the next hidden text or hyperlink, including **Show All** or **Hide All** at the top of a topic.	TAB
Select the previous hidden text or hyperlink.	SHIFT+TAB
Perform the action for the selected **Show All**, **Hide All**, hidden text, or hyperlink.	ENTER
Move back to the previous Help topic (**Back** button).	ALT+LEFT ARROW or BACKSPACE
Move forward to the next Help topic (**Forward** button).	ALT+RIGHT ARROW
Scroll small amounts up or down, respectively, within the currently displayed Help topic.	UP ARROW, DOWN ARROW

Scroll larger amounts up or down, respectively, within the currently displayed Help topic.	PAGE UP, PAGE DOWN
Display a menu of commands for the Help window. This requires that the Help window have the active focus (click in the Help window).	SHIFT+F10
Stop the last action (**Stop** button).	ESC
Refresh the window (**Refresh** button).	F5
Print the current Help topic. **Note:** If the cursor is not in the current Help topic, press F6 and then press CTRL+P.	CTRL+P
Change the connection state. You may need to press F6 more than once.	F6 (until the focus is in the **Type words to search for** box), TAB, DOWN ARROW
Type text in the **Type words to search for** box. You may need to press F6 more than once.	F6
Switch among areas in the Help window; for example, switch between the toolbar, **Type words to search for** box, and **Search** list.	F6
In a Table of Contents in tree view, select the next or previous item, respectively.	UP ARROW, DOWN ARROW

| In a Table of Contents in tree view, expand or collapse the selected item, respectively. | LEFT ARROW, RIGHT ARROW |

Microsoft Office Basics

Display and use windows

TASK	SHORTCUT
Switch to the next window.	ALT+TAB, TAB
Switch to the previous window.	ALT+SHIFT+TAB, TAB
Close the active window.	CTRL+W or CTRL+F4
Broadcast the open presentation to a remote audience using the PowerPoint web application.	CTRL+F5
Move to the next task pane from another pane in the program window (clockwise direction). You may need to press F6 more than once. **Note:** If pressing F6 does not display the task pane that you want, press ALT to put the focus on the Ribbon, and then press CTRL+TAB to move to the task pane.	F6
Move to a pane from another pane in the program window (counterclockwise direction).	SHIFT+F6
When more than one PowerPoint window is open, switch to the next PowerPoint window.	CTRL+F6

Switch to the previous PowerPoint window.	CTRL+SHIFT+F6
Copy a picture of the screen to the Clipboard.	PRINT SCREEN
Copy a picture of the selected window to the Clipboard.	ALT+PRINT SCREEN

Change or resize the font

Note: The cursor needs to be inside a text box to use these shortcuts.

TASK	SHORTCUT
Change the font.	CTRL+SHIFT+F
Change the font size.	CTRL+SHIFT+P
Increase the font size of the selected text.	CTRL+SHIFT+>
Decrease the font size of the selected text.	CTRL+SHIFT+<

Move around in text or cells

TASK	SHORTCUT
Move one character to the left.	LEFT ARROW
Move one character to the right.	RIGHT ARROW
Move one line up.	UP ARROW
Move one line down.	DOWN ARROW
Move one word to the left.	CTRL+LEFT ARROW
Move one word to the right.	CTRL+RIGHT ARROW
Move to the end of a line.	END
Move to the beginning of a line.	HOME

Move up one paragraph.	CTRL+UP ARROW
Move down one paragraph.	CTRL+DOWN ARROW
Move to the end of a text box.	CTRL+END
Move to the beginning of a text box.	CTRL+HOME
In Microsoft Office PowerPoint, move to the next title or body text placeholder. If it is the last placeholder on a slide, this will insert a new slide with the same slide layout as the original slide.	CTRL+ENTER
Repeat the last **Find** action.	SHIFT+F4

Find and replace

TASK	SHORTCUT
Open the **Find** dialog box.	CTRL+F
Open the **Replace** dialog box.	CTRL+H
Repeat the last **Find** action.	SHIFT+F4

Move around in and work in tables

TASK	SHORTCUT
Move to the next cell.	TAB
Move to the preceding cell.	SHIFT+TAB
Move to the next row.	DOWN ARROW
Move to the preceding row.	UP ARROW
Insert a tab in a cell.	CTRL+TAB
Start a new paragraph.	ENTER
Add a new row at the bottom of the table.	TAB at the end of the last row

Access and use task panes

TASK	SHORTCUT
Move to a task pane from another pane in the program window. (You may need to press F6 more than once.)	F6
When a task pane is active, select the next or previous option in the task pane, respectively.	TAB, SHIFT+TAB
Display the full set of commands on the task pane menu.	CTRL+DOWN ARROW
Move among choices on a selected submenu; move among certain options in a group of options in a dialog box.	DOWN ARROW or UP ARROW
Open the selected menu, or perform the action assigned to the selected button.	SPACEBAR or ENTER
Open a shortcut menu; open a drop-down menu for the selected gallery item.	SHIFT+F10
When a menu or submenu is visible, select the first or last command, respectively, on the menu or submenu.	HOME, END
Scroll up or down in the selected gallery list, respectively.	PAGE UP, PAGE DOWN
Move to the top or bottom of the selected gallery list, respectively.	HOME, END
Close a task pane.	CTRL+SPACEBAR, C
Open the Clipboard.	ALT+H, F, O

Resize a task pane

1. In the task pane, press CTRL+SPACEBAR to display a menu of additional commands.
2. Use the DOWN ARROW key to select the **Size** command, and then press ENTER.
3. Use the arrow keys to resize the task pane. Use CTRL+ the arrow keys to resize one pixel at a time.

Note: When you finish resizing, press ESC.

Use dialog boxes

TASK	SHORTCUT
Move to the next option or option group.	TAB
Move to the previous option or option group.	SHIFT+TAB
Switch to the next tab in a dialog box. (A tab must already be selected in an open dialog box)	DOWN ARROW
Switch to the previous tab in a dialog box. (A tab must already be selected in an open dialog box)	UP ARROW
Open a selected drop-down list.	DOWN ARROW, ALT+DOWN ARROW
Open the list if it is closed and move to an option in the list.	First letter of an option in a drop-down list
Move between options in an open drop-down list, or between options in a group of options.	UP ARROW, DOWN ARROW

Perform the action assigned to the selected button; select or clear the selected check box.	SPACEBAR
Select an option; select or clear a check box.	The letter underlined in an option
Perform the action assigned to a default button in a dialog box.	ENTER
Close a selected drop-down list; cancel a command and close a dialog box.	ESC

Use edit boxes within dialog boxes

An edit box is a blank box in which you type or paste an entry, such as your user name or the path of a folder.

TASK	SHORTCUT
Move to the beginning of the entry.	HOME
Move to the end of the entry.	END
Move one character to the left or right, respectively.	LEFT ARROW, RIGHT ARROW
Move one word to the left.	CTRL+LEFT ARROW
Move one word to the right.	CTRL+RIGHT ARROW
Select or cancel selection one character to the left.	SHIFT+LEFT ARROW
Select or cancel selection one character to the right.	SHIFT+RIGHT ARROW
Select or cancel selection one word to the left.	CTRL+SHIFT+LEFT ARROW
Select or cancel selection one word to the right.	CTRL+SHIFT+RIGHT ARROW
Select from the cursor to the beginning of the entry.	SHIFT+HOME

Select from the cursor to the end of the entry.	SHIFT+END

Use the Open and Save As dialog boxes

TASK	SHORTCUT
Open the Open dialog box	ALT+F then O
Open the Save As dialog box	ALT+F then A
Move between options in an open drop-down list, or between options in a group of options	Arrow keys
Display a shortcut menu for a selected item, such as a folder or file.	SHIFT+F10
Move between options or areas in the dialog box.	TAB
Open the filepath drop-down menu	F4 or ALT+I
Refresh the file list.	F5

Navigating The Ribbon

Access any command with a few keystrokes

1. Press ALT.

   The KeyTips are displayed over each feature that is available in the current view.

2. Press the letter shown in the KeyTip over the feature that you want to use.
3. Depending on which letter you press, you may be shown additional KeyTips. For example, if the **Home** tab is active and you press N, the **Insert** tab is displayed, along with the KeyTips for the groups on that tab.

4. Continue pressing letters until you press the letter of the command or control that you want to use. In some cases, you must first press the letter of the group that contains the command. For example, if the **Home** tab is active, press ALT+H, F, S will take you to the **Size** list box in the **Font** group.

Note: To cancel the action that you are taking and hide the KeyTips, press ALT.

Change the keyboard focus without using the mouse

Another way to use the keyboard to work with the Ribbon is to move the focus among the tabs and commands until you find the feature that you want to use. The following table lists some ways to move the keyboard focus without using the mouse.

TASK	SHORTCUT
Select the active tab of the Ribbon and activate the access keys.	ALT or F10. Press either of these keys again to move back to the document and cancel the access keys.
Move left or right to another tab of the Ribbon, respectively.	F10 to select the active tab, and then LEFT ARROW, RIGHT ARROW
Hide or show the Ribbon.	CTRL+F1
Display the shortcut menu for the selected command.	SHIFT+F10

Move the focus to select each of the following areas of the window: • Active tab of the Ribbon • Any open task panes • Your document	F6
Move the focus to each command on the Ribbon, forward or backward respectively.	TAB, SHIFT+TAB
Move down, up, left, or right among the items on the Ribbon, respectively.	DOWN ARROW, UP ARROW, LEFT ARROW, RIGHT ARROW
Activate the selected command or control on the Ribbon.	SPACE BAR or ENTER
Open the selected menu or gallery on the Ribbon.	SPACE BAR or ENTER
Activate a command or control on the Ribbon so you can modify a value.	ENTER
Finish modifying a value in a control on the Ribbon, and move the focus back to the document.	ENTER
Get help on the selected command or control on the Ribbon. (If no Help topic is associated with the selected command, a general Help topic about the program is shown instead.)	F1

Common Tasks In Microsoft Office PowerPoint

Move between panes

TASK	SHORTCUT
Move clockwise among panes in Normal view.	F6
Move counterclockwise among panes in Normal view.	SHIFT+F6
Switch between **Slides** and **Outline** tabs in the Outline and Slides pane in Normal view.	CTRL+SHIFT+TAB

Insert A SmartArt Graphic In An Office Document

1. In the Microsoft Office program where you want to insert the graphic, press Alt, then N, and then M to open the **SmartArt Graphic** dialog box.
2. Press Up Arrow or Down Arrow to select the type of graphic that you want.
3. Press Tab to move to the Layout task pane.
4. Press the arrow keys to select the layout that you want.
5. Press Enter to insert the selected layout.

Work With Shapes In A SmartArt Graphic.

TASK	SHORTCUT
Select the next element in a SmartArt graphic.	Tab
Select the previous element in a SmartArt graphic.	Shift+Tab

Select all shapes.	Ctrl +A
Remove focus from the selected shape.	Esc
Nudge the selected shape up.	Up Arrow
Nudge the selected shape down.	Down Arrow
Nudge the selected shape left.	Left Arrow
Nudge the selected shape right.	Right Arrow
Edit text in the selected shape.	Enter or F2, Esc to exit shape
Delete the selected shape.	Delete or Backspace
Cut the selected shape.	Ctrl+X or Shift+Delete
Copy the selected shape.	Ctrl+C
Paste the contents of the Clipboard.	Ctrl+V
Undo the last action.	Ctrl+Z

Move And Resize Shapes In A SmartArt Graphic.

TASK	SHORTCUT
Enlarge the selected shape horizontally.	Shift+Right Arrow
Reduce the selected shape horizontally.	Shift+Left Arrow
Enlarge the selected shape vertically.	Shift+Up Arrow
Reduce the selected shape vertically.	Shift+Down Arrow
Rotate the selected shape to the right.	Alt+Right Arrow
Rotate the selected shape to the left.	Alt+Left Arrow

Notes:

- To apply more precise adjustments to shapes, press the Ctrl key in addition to any of the above keyboard shortcuts.
- These keyboard shortcuts apply to multiple selections as if you selected each item individually.

Work With Text In A SmartArt Graphic

TASK	SHORTCUT
Move one character to the left.	Left Arrow
Move one character to the right.	Right Arrow
Move up one line.	Up Arrow
Move down one line.	Down Arrow
Move one word to the left.	Ctrl+Left Arrow
Move one word to the right.	Ctrl+Right Arrow
Move one paragraph up.	Ctrl+Up Arrow
Move one paragraph down.	Ctrl+Down Arrow
Move to the end of a line.	End
Move to the beginning of a line.	Home
Move to the end of a text box.	Ctrl+End
Move to the beginning of a text box.	Ctrl+Home
Cut selected text.	Ctrl+X
Copy selected text.	Ctrl+C
Paste selected text.	Ctrl+V
Move the selected text up.	Alt+Shift+Up Arrow
Move the selected text down.	Alt+Shift+Down Arrow
Undo the last action.	Ctrl+Z
Delete one character to the left.	Backspace
Delete one word to the left.	Ctrl+Backspace
Delete one character to the right.	Delete
Delete one word to the right.	Ctrl+Delete
Promote the selected text.	Alt+Shift+Left Arrow

Demote the selected text.	Alt+Shift+Right Arrow
Check the spelling (not available in Word).	F7

Apply Character Formatting

TASK	SHORTCUT
Open the **Font** dialog box.	Ctrl+Shift+F or Ctrl+Shift+P
Increase the font size of the selected text.	Ctrl+Shift+>
Decrease the font size of the selected text.	Ctrl+Shift+<
Switch the case of selected text (lower case, Title Case, UPPER CASE).	Shift+F3
Apply bold formatting to the selected text.	Ctrl+B
Apply an underline to the selected text.	Ctrl+U
Apply italic formatting to the selected text.	Ctrl+I
Apply subscript formatting to the selected text.	Ctrl+Equal Sign
Apply superscript formatting to the selected text.	Ctrl+Shift+Plus Sign
Adjust the superscript/subscript offset up.	Ctrl+Alt+Shift+>
Adjust the superscript/subscript offset down.	Ctrl+Alt+Shift+<

Remove all character formatting from the selected text.	Shift+Ctrl+Spacebar

Copy Text Formatting

TASK	SHORTCUT
Copy formatting from the selected text.	Shift+Ctrl+C
Paste formatting to the selected text.	Shift+Ctrl+V

Apply Paragraph Formatting

TASK	SHORTCUT
Center a paragraph.	Ctrl+E
Justify a paragraph.	Ctrl+J
Left align a paragraph.	Ctrl+L
Right align a paragraph.	Ctrl+R
Demote a bullet point.	Tab or Alt+Shift+Right Arrow
Promote a bullet point.	Shift+Tab or Alt+Shift+Left Arrow

Use The Text Pane

TASK	SHORTCUT
Merge two lines of text.	Delete at the end of the first line of text
Display the shortcut menu.	Shift+F10
Switch between the **Text** pane and the drawing canvas.	Ctrl+Shift+F2
Close the **Text** pane.	Alt+F4
Switch the focus from the **Text** pane to the border of the SmartArt graphic.	Esc

Open the SmartArt graphics Help topic. (Your pointer should be in the Text pane.)	Ctrl +Shift+F1

Work In An Outline

TASK	SHORTCUT
Promote a paragraph.	ALT+SHIFT+LEFT ARROW
Demote a paragraph.	ALT+SHIFT+RIGHT ARROW
Move selected paragraphs up.	ALT+SHIFT+UP ARROW
Move selected paragraphs down.	ALT+SHIFT+DOWN ARROW
Show heading level 1.	ALT+SHIFT+1
Expand text below a heading.	ALT+SHIFT+PLUS SIGN
Collapse text below a heading.	ALT+SHIFT+MINUS SIGN

Work with shapes, pictures, boxes, objects, and WordArt

Insert a shape

1. Press and release ALT, then N, then S, then H to select **Shapes**.
2. Use the arrow keys to move through the categories of shapes, and select the shape that you want.
3. Press CTRL+ENTER to insert the shape that you selected.

Insert a text box

1. Press and release ALT, then N, and then X.
2. Press CTRL+ENTER to insert the text box.

Insert an object

1. Press and release ALT, then N, then J to select **Object**.
2. Use the arrow keys to move through the objects.
3. Press CTRL+ENTER to insert the object that you want.

Insert WordArt

1. Press and release ALT, then N, then W to select **WordArt**.
2. Use the arrow keys to select the WordArt style that you want, and then press ENTER.
3. Type the text that you want.

Select a shape

Note: If your cursor is within text, press ESC.

- To select a single shape, press the TAB key to cycle forward (or SHIFT+TAB to cycle backward) through the objects until sizing handles appear on the object that you want to select.
- To select multiple items, use the selection pane.

Group or ungroup shapes, pictures, and WordArt objects

- To group shapes, pictures, or WordArt objects, select the items that you want to group, and then press CTRL+G.

- To ungroup a group, select the group, and then press CTRL+SHIFT+G.

Show or hide a grid or guides

TASK	SHORTCUT
Show or hide the grid.	SHIFT+F9
Show or hide guides.	ALT+F9

Copy the attributes of a shape

1. Select the shape with the attributes that you want to copy.

   Note: If you select a shape with text, you copy the look and style of the text in addition to the attributes of the shape.

2. Press CTRL+SHIFT+C to copy the object attributes.
3. Press the TAB key or SHIFT+TAB to select the object that you want to copy the attributes to.
4. Press CTRL+SHIFT+V.

Select text and objects

TASK	SHORTCUT
Select one character to the right.	SHIFT+RIGHT ARROW
Select one character to the left.	SHIFT+LEFT ARROW
Select to the end of a word.	CTRL+SHIFT+RIGHT ARROW
Select to the beginning of a word.	CTRL+SHIFT+LEFT ARROW

Select one line up (with the cursor at the beginning of a line).	SHIFT+UP ARROW
Select one line down (with the cursor at the beginning of a line).	SHIFT+DOWN ARROW
Select an object (when the text inside the object is selected).	ESC
Select another object (when one object is selected).	TAB or SHIFT+TAB until the object you want is selected
Select text within an object (with an object selected).	ENTER
Select all objects.	CTRL+A (on the **Slides** tab)
Select all slides.	CTRL+A (in Slide Sorter view)
Select all text.	CTRL+A (on the **Outline** tab)

Delete and copy text and objects

TASK	SHORTCUT
Delete one character to the left.	BACKSPACE
Delete one word to the left.	CTRL+BACKSPACE
Delete one character to the right.	DELETE
Delete one word to the right. **Note:** The cursor must be between words to do this.	CTRL+DELETE
Cut selected object or text.	CTRL+X
Copy selected object or text.	CTRL+C
Paste cut or copied object or text.	CTRL+V
Undo the last action.	CTRL+Z
Redo the last action.	CTRL+Y

Copy formatting only.	CTRL+SHIFT+C
Paste formatting only.	CTRL+SHIFT+V
Open **Paste Special** dialog box.	CTRL+ALT+V

Move around in text

TASK	SHORTCUT
Move one character to the left.	LEFT ARROW
Move one character to the right.	RIGHT ARROW
Move one line up.	UP ARROW
Move one line down.	DOWN ARROW
Move one word to the left.	CTRL+LEFT ARROW
Move one word to the right.	CTRL+RIGHT ARROW
Move to the end of a line.	END
Move to the beginning of a line.	HOME
Move up one paragraph.	CTRL+UP ARROW
Move down one paragraph.	CTRL+DOWN ARROW
Move to the end of a text box.	CTRL+END
Move to the beginning of a text box.	CTRL+HOME
Move to the next title or body text placeholder. If it is the last placeholder on a slide, this will insert a new slide with the same slide layout as the original slide.	CTRL+ENTER
Move to repeat the last **Find** action.	SHIFT+F4

Move around in and work on tables

TASK	SHORTCUT
Move to the next cell.	TAB

Move to the preceding cell.	SHIFT+TAB
Move to the next row.	DOWN ARROW
Move to the preceding row.	UP ARROW
Insert a tab in a cell.	CTRL+TAB
Start a new paragraph.	ENTER
Add a new row at the bottom of the table.	TAB at the end of the last row

Edit a linked or embedded object

1. Press TAB OR SHIFT+TAB to select the object that you want.
2. Press SHIFT+F10 for the shortcut menu.
3. Use the DOWN ARROW until **Worksheet Object** is selected, press RIGHT ARROW to select **Edit**, and press ENTER.

   Note: The name of the command in the shortcut menu depends on the type of embedded or linked object. For example, an embedded Microsoft Office Excel worksheet has the command **Worksheet Object**, whereas an embedded Microsoft Office Visio Drawing has the command **Visio Object**.

Format and align characters and paragraphs

Change or resize the font

Note: You must first select the text that you wish to change to use these keyboard shortcuts.

TASK	SHORTCUT
Open the **Font** dialog box to change the font.	CTRL+SHIFT+F
Increase the font size.	CTRL+SHIFT+>

| Decrease the font size. | CTRL+SHIFT+< |

Apply character formats

TASK	SHORTCUT
Open the **Font** dialog box to change the formatting of characters.	CTRL+T
Change the case of letters between sentence, lowercase, or uppercase.	SHIFT+F3
Apply bold formatting.	CTRL+B
Apply an underline.	CTRL+U
Apply italic formatting.	CTRL+I
Apply subscript formatting (automatic spacing).	CTRL+EQUAL SIGN
Apply superscript formatting (automatic spacing).	CTRL+SHIFT+PLUS SIGN
Remove manual character formatting, such as subscript and superscript.	CTRL+SPACEBAR
Insert a hyperlink.	CTRL+K

Copy text formats

TASK	SHORTCUT
Copy formats.	CTRL+SHIFT+C
Paste formats.	CTRL+SHIFT+V

Align paragraphs

TASK	SHORTCUT
Center a paragraph.	CTRL+E
Justify a paragraph.	CTRL+J
Left align a paragraph.	CTRL+L

| Right align a paragraph. | CTRL+R |

Run A Presentation

You can use the following keyboard shortcuts while you are running your presentation in Slide Show view.

Slide Show Shortcuts

TASK	SHORTCUT
Start a presentation from the beginning.	F5
Perform the next animation or advance to the next slide.	N, ENTER, PAGE DOWN, RIGHT ARROW, DOWN ARROW, or SPACEBAR
Perform the previous animation or return to the previous slide.	P, PAGE UP, LEFT ARROW, UP ARROW, or BACKSPACE
Go to slide number.	number+ENTER
Display a blank black slide, or return to the presentation from a blank black slide.	B or PERIOD
Display a blank white slide, or return to the presentation from a blank white slide.	W or COMMA
Stop or restart an automatic presentation.	S
End a presentation.	ESC or HYPHEN
Erase on-screen annotations.	E
Go to the next slide, if the next slide is hidden.	H

Set new timings while rehearsing.	T
Use original timings while rehearsing.	O
Use mouse-click to advance while rehearsing.	M
Re-record slide narration and timing	R
Return to the first slide.	Press and hold Right and Left Mouse buttons for 2 seconds
Show or hide the arrow pointer	A or =
Change the pointer to a pen.	CTRL+P
Change the pointer to an arrow.	CTRL+A
Change the pointer to an eraser	CTRL+E
Show or hide ink markup	CTRL+M
Hide the pointer and navigation button immediately.	CTRL+H
Hide the pointer and navigation button in 15 seconds.	CTRL+U
View the All Slides dialog box	CTRL+S
View the computer task bar	CTRL+T
Display the shortcut menu.	SHIFT+F10
Go to the first or next hyperlink on a slide.	TAB

Go to the last or previous hyperlink on a slide.	SHIFT+TAB
Perform the "mouse click" behavior of the selected hyperlink.	ENTER while a hyperlink is selected

Media Shortcuts During Presentation

TASK	SHORTCUT
Stop media playback	ALT+Q
Toggle between play and pause	ALT+P
Go to the next bookmark	ALT+END
Go to the previous bookmark	ALT+HOME
Increase the sound volume	ALT+Up
Decrease the sound volume	ALT+Down
Seek forward	ALT+SHIFT+PAGE DOWN
Seek backward	ALT+SHIFT+PAGE UP
Mute the sound	ALT+U

Tip: You can press F1 during your presentation to see a list of controls.

Browse Web presentations

The following keys are for viewing your Web presentation in Microsoft Internet Explorer 4.0 or later.

TASK	SHORTCUT
Move forward through the hyperlinks in a Web presentation, the Address bar, and the Links bar.	TAB
Move back through the hyperlinks in a Web presentation, the Address bar, and the Links bar.	SHIFT+TAB
Perform the "mouse click" behavior of the selected hyperlink.	ENTER
Go to the next slide.	SPACEBAR

Use the Selection pane feature

Use the following keyboard shortcuts in the Selection pane.

To launch the Selection pane, press Alt, then H, then S, then L, and then P.

TASK	SHORTCUT
Cycle the focus through the different panes.	F6
Display the context menu.	SHIFT+F10
Move the focus to a single item or group.	UP ARROW or DOWN ARROW
Move the focus from an item in a group to its parent group.	LEFT ARROW
Move the focus from a group to the first item in that group.	RIGHT ARROW
Expand a focused group and all its child groups.	* (on numeric keypad only)
Expand a focused group.	+ (on numeric keypad only)
Collapse a focused group.	- (on numeric keypad only)

Move the focus to an item and select it.	SHIFT+UP ARROW or SHIFT+DOWN ARROW
Select a focused item.	SPACEBAR or ENTER
Cancel selection of a focused item.	SHIFT+SPACEBAR or SHIFT+ENTER
Move a selected item forward.	CTRL+SHIFT+F
Move a selected item backward.	CTRL+SHIFT+B
Show or hide a focused item.	CTRL+SHIFT+S
Rename a focused item.	F2
Switch the keyboard focus within the Selection pane between tree view and the **Show All** and **Hide All** buttons.	TAB or SHIFT+TAB
Collapse all groups. **Note:** The focus must be in the tree view of the Selection pane to use this shortcut.	ALT+SHIFT+1
Expand all groups.	ALT+SHIFT+9

Tip: You can press F1 during your presentation to see a list of controls.

CHAPTER 4

Keyboard Shortcuts for Microsoft Word 2010.

Definition of Program: Microsoft Word is a word processing program designed in 1983 by Microsoft Corporation. It allows users to create and modify simple and sophisticated documents.

Note: If you are using Microsoft Word Starter, be aware that not all the features listed in this chapter for Word are supported in Word Starter.

The following keyboard shortcuts will help you become a successful user of Microsoft Word 2010.

Microsoft Office Basics

Display And Use Windows

TASK	SHORTCUT
Switch to the next window.	ALT+TAB
Switch to the previous window.	ALT+SHIFT+TAB
Close the active window.	CTRL+W or CTRL+F4
Restore the size of the active window after you maximize it.	ALT+F5
Move to a task pane from another pane in the program window (clockwise direction). You may need to press F6 more than once.	F6

Move to a task pane from another pane in the program window (counterclockwise direction).	SHIFT+F6
When more than one window is open, switch to the next window.	CTRL+F6
Switch to the previous window.	CTRL+SHIFT+F6
Maximize or restore a selected window.	CTRL+F10
Copy a picture of the screen to the Clipboard.	PRINT SCREEN
Copy a picture of the selected window to the Clipboard.	ALT+PRINT SCREEN

Use Dialog Boxes

TASK	SHORTCUT
Move to the next option or option group.	TAB
Move to the previous option or option group.	SHIFT+TAB
Switch to the next tab in a dialog box.	CTRL+TAB
Switch to the previous tab in a dialog box.	CTRL+SHIFT+TAB
Move between options in an open drop-down list, or between options in a group of options.	Arrow keys
Perform the action assigned to the selected button; select or clear the selected check box.	SPACEBAR
Select an option; select or clear a check box.	ALT+ the letter underlined in an option

Open a selected drop-down list.	ALT+DOWN ARROW
Select an option from a drop-down list.	First letter of an option in a drop-down list
Close a selected drop-down list; cancel a command and close a dialog box.	ESC
Run the selected command.	ENTER

Use edit boxes within dialog boxes

An edit box is a blank in which you type or paste an entry, such as your user name or the path of a folder.

TASK	SHORTCUT
Move to the beginning of the entry.	HOME
Move to the end of the entry.	END
Move one character to the left or right.	LEFT ARROW or RIGHT ARROW
Move one word to the left.	CTRL+LEFT ARROW
Move one word to the right.	CTRL+RIGHT ARROW
Select or unselect one character to the left.	SHIFT+LEFT ARROW
Select or unselect one character to the right.	SHIFT+RIGHT ARROW
Select or unselect one word to the left.	CTRL+SHIFT+LEFT ARROW
Select or unselect one word to the right.	CTRL+SHIFT+RIGHT ARROW
Select from the insertion point to the beginning of the entry.	SHIFT+HOME

Select from the insertion point to the end of the entry.	SHIFT+END

Use the Open and Save As dialog boxes

TASK	SHORTCUT
Display the **Open** dialog box.	CTRL+F12 or CTRL+O
Display the **Save As** dialog box.	F12
Open the selected folder or file.	ENTER
Open the folder one level above the selected folder.	BACKSPACE
Delete the selected folder or file.	DELETE
Display a shortcut menu for a selected item such as a folder or file.	SHIFT+F10
Move forward through options.	TAB
Move back through options.	SHIFT+TAB
Open the **Look in** list.	F4 or ALT+I

Undo and redo actions

TASK	SHORTCUT
Cancel an action.	ESC
Undo an action.	CTRL+Z
Redo or repeat an action.	CTRL+Y

Access and use task panes and galleries

TASK	SHORTCUT
Move to a task pane from another pane in the program window. (You may need to press F6 more than once.)	F6

When a menu is active, move to a task pane. (You may need to press CTRL+TAB more than once.)	CTRL+TAB
When a task pane is active, select the next or previous option in the task pane.	TAB or SHIFT+TAB
Display the full set of commands on the task pane menu.	CTRL+SPACEBAR
Perform the action assigned to the selected button.	SPACEBAR or ENTER
Open a drop-down menu for the selected gallery item.	SHIFT+F10
Select the first or last item in a gallery.	HOME or END
Scroll up or down in the selected gallery list.	PAGE UP or PAGE DOWN

Close a task pane

1. Press F6 to move to the task pane, if necessary.
2. Press CTRL+SPACEBAR.
3. Use the arrow keys to select **Close**, and then press ENTER.

Move a task pane

1. Press F6 to move to the task pane, if necessary.
2. Press CTRL+SPACEBAR.
3. Use the arrow keys to select **Move**, and then press ENTER.
4. Use the arrow keys to move the task pane, and then press ENTER.

Resize a task pane

1. Press F6 to move to the task pane, if necessary.
2. Press CTRL+SPACEBAR.
3. Use the arrow keys to select **Size**, and then press ENTER.
4. Use the arrow keys to resize the task pane, and then press ENTER.

Access and use available actions

TASK	SHORTCUT
Display the shortcut menu for the selected item.	SHIFT+F10
Display the menu or message for an available action or for the AutoCorrect Options button ![]. If more than one action is present, switch to the next action and display its menu or message.	ALT+SHIFT+F10
Move between options in a menu of available actions.	Arrow keys
Perform the action for the selected item on a menu of available actions.	ENTER
Close the available actions menu or message.	ESC

Tips

- You can ask to be notified by a sound whenever an action is available (not available in Word Starter). To hear audio cues, you must have a sound card. You must also have Microsoft Office Sounds installed on your computer.

- If you have access to the Internet, you can download Microsoft Office Sounds from Office.com. After you install the sound files, do the following:
    a. Press ALT+F, T to open **Word Options**.
    b. Press A to select **Advanced**, and then press TAB to move to the **Advanced Options for working with Word** .
    c. Press ALT+S twice to move to the **Provide feedback with sound** check box, which is under **General**, and then press SPACEBAR.
    d. Press TAB repeatedly to select **OK**, and then press ENTER.

    Note: When you select or clear this check box, the setting affects all Office programs that support sound.

Navigating The Ribbon

Access any command with a few keystrokes

Access keys let you quickly use a command by pressing a few keys, regardless of where you are in the program. Every command in Word 2010 can be accessed by using an access key. You can get to most commands by using two to five keystrokes. To use an access key:

1. Press ALT.

    The KeyTips are displayed over each feature that is available in the current view.

2. Press the letter shown in the KeyTip over the feature that you want to use.

3. Depending on which letter you press, you may be shown additional KeyTips. For example, if the **Home** tab is active and you press N, the **Insert** tab is displayed, along with the KeyTips for the groups on that tab.

4. Continue pressing letters until you press the letter of the command or control that you want to use. In some cases, you must first press the letter of the group that contains the command.

Note: To cancel the action that you are taking and hide the KeyTips, press ALT.

Change the keyboard focus without using the mouse

Another way to use the keyboard to work with programs that feature the Office Ribbon is to move the focus among the tabs and commands until you find the feature that you want to use. The following table lists some ways to move the keyboard focus without using the mouse.

TASK	SHORTCUT
Select the active tab of the Ribbon and activate the access keys.	ALT or F10. Press either of these keys again to move back to the document and cancel the access keys.
Move to another tab of the Ribbon.	F10 to select the active tab, and then LEFT ARROW or RIGHT ARROW
Expand or collapse the Ribbon.	CTRL+F1
Display the shortcut menu for the selected item.	SHIFT+F10

Move the focus to select each of the following areas of the window: • Active tab of the Ribbon • Any open task panes • Status bar at the bottom of the window • Your document	F6
Move the focus to each command on the Ribbon, forward or backward, respectively.	TAB or SHIFT+TAB
Move down, up, left, or right, respectively, among the items on the Ribbon.	DOWN ARROW, UP ARROW, LEFT ARROW, or RIGHT ARROW
Activate the selected command or control on the Ribbon.	SPACEBAR or ENTER
Open the selected menu or gallery on the Ribbon.	SPACEBAR or ENTER
Activate a command or control on the Ribbon so you can modify a value.	ENTER
Finish modifying a value in a control on the Ribbon, and move focus back to the document.	ENTER
Get help on the selected command or control on the Ribbon. (If no Help topic is associated with the selected command, a general Help topic	F1

about the program is shown instead.)	

Quick Reference For Microsoft Word

Common Tasks in Microsoft Word

TASK	SHORTCUT
Create a nonbreaking space.	CTRL+SHIFT+SPACEBAR
Create a nonbreaking hyphen.	CTRL+SHIFT+HYPHEN
Make letters bold.	CTRL+B
Make letters italic.	CTRL+I
Make letters underline.	CTRL+U
Decrease font size one value.	CTRL+SHIFT+<
Increase font size one value.	CTRL+SHIFT+>
Decrease font size 1 point.	CTRL+[
Increase font size 1 point.	CTRL+]
Remove paragraph or character formatting.	CTRL+SPACEBAR
Copy the selected text or object.	CTRL+C
Cut the selected text or object.	CTRL+X
Paste text or an object.	CTRL+V
Paste special	CTRL+ALT+V
Paste formatting only	CTRL+SHIFT+V
Undo the last action.	CTRL+Z
Redo the last action.	CTRL+Y

Open the **Word Count** dialog box.	CTRL+SHIFT+G

Working with documents and Web pages

Create, view, and save documents

TASK	SHORTCUT
Create a new document.	CTRL+N
Open a document.	CTRL+O
Close a document.	CTRL+W
Split the document window.	ALT+CTRL+S
Remove the document window split.	ALT+SHIFT+C or ALT+CTRL+S
Save a document.	CTRL+S

Find, replace, and browse through text

TASK	SHORTCUT
Open the **Navigation** task pane (to search document).	CTRL+F
Repeat find (after closing **Find and Replace** window).	ALT+CTRL+Y
Replace text, specific formatting, and special items.	CTRL+H
Go to a page, bookmark, footnote, table, comment, graphic, or other location.	CTRL+G
Switch between the last four places that you have edited.	ALT+CTRL+Z
Open a list of browse options. Press the arrow keys to select an option, and then press ENTER to	ALT+CTRL+HOME

browse through a document by using the selected option.	
Move to the previous browse object (set in browse options).	CTRL+PAGE UP
Move to the next browse object (set in browse options).	CTRL+PAGE DOWN

Switch to Another View

TASK	SHORTCUT
Switch to Print Layout view.	ALT+CTRL+P
Switch to Outline view.	ALT+CTRL+O
Switch to Draft view.	ALT+CTRL+N

Outline view

TASK	SHORTCUT
Promote a paragraph.	ALT+SHIFT+LEFT ARROW
Demote a paragraph.	ALT+SHIFT+RIGHT ARROW
Demote to body text.	CTRL+SHIFT+N
Move selected paragraphs up.	ALT+SHIFT+UP ARROW
Move selected paragraphs down.	ALT+SHIFT+DOWN ARROW
Expand text under a heading.	ALT+SHIFT+PLUS SIGN
Collapse text under a heading.	ALT+SHIFT+MINUS SIGN
Expand or collapse all text or headings.	ALT+SHIFT+A
Hide or display character formatting.	The slash (/) key on the numeric keypad
Show the first line of body text or all body text.	ALT+SHIFT+L

Show all headings with the Heading 1 style.	ALT+SHIFT+1
Show all headings up to Heading n.	ALT+SHIFT+n
Insert a tab character.	CTRL+TAB

Print and preview documents

TASK	SHORTCUT
Print a document.	CTRL+P
Switch to print preview.	ALT+CTRL+I
Move around the preview page when zoomed in.	Arrow keys
Move by one preview page when zoomed out.	PAGE UP or PAGE DOWN
Move to the first preview page when zoomed out.	CTRL+HOME
Move to the last preview page when zoomed out.	CTRL+END

Review documents

TASK	SHORTCUT
Insert a comment.	ALT+CTRL+M
Turn change tracking on or off.	CTRL+SHIFT+E
Close the Reviewing Pane if it is open.	ALT+SHIFT+C

Full Screen Reading view

Note: Some screen readers may not be compatible with Full Screen Reading view.

TASK	SHORTCUT
Go to beginning of document.	HOME
Go to end of document.	END

Go to page n.	n, ENTER
Exit reading layout view.	ESC

References, Footnotes, and Endnotes

TASK	SHORTCUT
Mark a table of contents entry.	ALT+SHIFT+O
Mark a table of authorities entry (citation).	ALT+SHIFT+I
Mark an index entry.	ALT+SHIFT+X
Insert a footnote.	ALT+CTRL+F
Insert an endnote.	ALT+CTRL+D

Work With Web Pages

TASK	SHORTCUT
Insert a hyperlink.	CTRL+K
Go back one page.	ALT+LEFT ARROW
Go forward one page.	ALT+RIGHT ARROW
Refresh.	F9

Edit and move text and graphics

Delete text and graphics

TASK	SHORTCUT
Delete one character to the left.	BACKSPACE
Delete one word to the left.	CTRL+BACKSPACE
Delete one character to the right.	DELETE
Delete one word to the right.	CTRL+DELETE
Cut selected text to the Office Clipboard.	CTRL+X
Undo the last action.	CTRL+Z
Cut to the Spike.	CTRL+F3

Copy and Move Text and Graphics

TASK	SHORTCUT
Open the Office Clipboard	Press ALT+H to move to the **Home** tab, and then press F,O.
Copy selected text or graphics to the Office Clipboard.	CTRL+C
Cut selected text or graphics to the Office Clipboard.	CTRL+X
Paste the most recent addition or pasted item from the Office Clipboard.	CTRL+V
Move text or graphics once.	F2 (then move the cursor and press ENTER)
Copy text or graphics once.	SHIFT+F2 (then move the cursor and press ENTER)
When text or an object is selected, open the **Create New Building Block** dialog box.	ALT+F3
When the building block — for example, a SmartArt graphic — is selected, display the shortcut menu that is associated with it.	SHIFT+F10
Cut to the Spike.	CTRL+F3
Paste the Spike contents.	CTRL+SHIFT+F3
Copy the header or footer used in the previous section of the document.	ALT+SHIFT+R

Insert Special Characters

TASK	SHORTCUT
A field	CTRL+F9
A line break	SHIFT+ENTER
A page break	CTRL+ENTER
A column break	CTRL+SHIFT+ENTER
An em dash	ALT+CTRL+MINUS SIGN
An en dash	CTRL+MINUS SIGN
An optional hyphen	CTRL+HYPHEN
A nonbreaking hyphen	CTRL+SHIFT+HYPHEN
A nonbreaking space	CTRL+SHIFT+SPACEBAR
The copyright symbol	ALT+CTRL+C
The registered trademark symbol	ALT+CTRL+R
The trademark symbol	ALT+CTRL+T
An ellipsis	ALT+CTRL+PERIOD
A single opening quotation mark	CTRL+`(single quotation mark), `(single quotation mark)
A single closing quotation mark	CTRL+' (single quotation mark), ' (single quotation mark)
Double opening quotation marks	CTRL+` (single quotation mark), SHIFT+' (single quotation mark)

Double closing quotation marks	CTRL+' (single quotation mark), SHIFT+' (single quotation mark)
An AutoText entry	ENTER (after you type the first few characters of the AutoText entry name and when the ScreenTip appears)

Insert Characters By Using Character Codes

TASK	SHORTCUT
Insert the Unicode character for the specified Unicode (hexadecimal) character code. For example, to insert the euro currency symbol (€), type **20AC**, and then hold down ALT and press X.	The character code, ALT+X
Find out the Unicode character code for the selected character	ALT+X
Insert the ANSI character for the specified ANSI (decimal) character code. For example, to insert the euro currency symbol, hold down ALT and press 0128 on the numeric keypad.	ALT+the character code (on the numeric keypad)

Select Text and Graphics

Select text by holding down SHIFT and using the arrow keys to move the cursor.

Extend a selection

TASK	SHORTCUT
Turn extend mode on.	F8

Select the nearest character.	F8, and then press LEFT ARROW or RIGHT ARROW
Increase the size of a selection.	F8 (press once to select a word, twice to select a sentence, and so on)
Reduce the size of a selection.	SHIFT+F8
Turn extend mode off.	ESC
Extend a selection one character to the right.	SHIFT+RIGHT ARROW
Extend a selection one character to the left.	SHIFT+LEFT ARROW
Extend a selection to the end of a word.	CTRL+SHIFT+RIGHT ARROW
Extend a selection to the beginning of a word.	CTRL+SHIFT+LEFT ARROW
Extend a selection to the end of a line.	SHIFT+END
Extend a selection to the beginning of a line.	SHIFT+HOME
Extend a selection one line down.	SHIFT+DOWN ARROW
Extend a selection one line up.	SHIFT+UP ARROW
Extend a selection to the end of a paragraph.	CTRL+SHIFT+DOWN ARROW

Extend a selection to the beginning of a paragraph.	CTRL+SHIFT+UP ARROW
Extend a selection one screen down.	SHIFT+PAGE DOWN
Extend a selection one screen up.	SHIFT+PAGE UP
Extend a selection to the beginning of a document.	CTRL+SHIFT+HOME
Extend a selection to the end of a document.	CTRL+SHIFT+END
Extend a selection to the end of a window.	ALT+CTRL+SHIFT+PAGE DOWN
Extend a selection to include the entire document.	CTRL+A
Select a vertical block of text.	CTRL+SHIFT+F8, and then use the arrow keys; press ESC to cancel selection mode
Extend a selection to a specific location in a document.	F8+arrow keys; press ESC to cancel selection mode

Select text and graphics in a table

TASK	SHORTCUT
Select the next cell's contents.	TAB
Select the preceding cell's contents.	SHIFT+TAB

Extend a selection to adjacent cells.	Hold down SHIFT and press an arrow key repeatedly
Select a column.	Use the arrow keys to move to the column's top or bottom cell, and then do one of the following: • Press SHIFT+ALT+PAGE DOWN to select the column from top to bottom. • Press SHIFT+ALT+PAGE UP to select the column from bottom to top.
Extend a selection (or block).	CTRL+SHIFT+F8, and then use the arrow keys; press ESC to cancel selection mode
Select an entire table.	ALT+5 on the numeric keypad (with NUM LOCK off)

Move Through Your Document

TASK	SHORTCUT
One character to the left	LEFT ARROW
One character to the right	RIGHT ARROW
One word to the left	CTRL+LEFT ARROW
One word to the right	CTRL+RIGHT ARROW
One paragraph up	CTRL+UP ARROW
One paragraph down	CTRL+DOWN ARROW
One cell to the left (in a table)	SHIFT+TAB
One cell to the right (in a table)	TAB

Up one line	UP ARROW
Down one line	DOWN ARROW
To the end of a line	END
To the beginning of a line	HOME
To the top of the window	ALT+CTRL+PAGE UP
To the end of the window	ALT+CTRL+PAGE DOWN
Up one screen (scrolling)	PAGE UP
Down one screen (scrolling)	PAGE DOWN
To the top of the next page	CTRL+PAGE DOWN
To the top of the previous page	CTRL+PAGE UP
To the end of a document	CTRL+END
To the beginning of a document	CTRL+HOME
To a previous revision	SHIFT+F5
After opening a document, to the location you were working in when the document was last closed	SHIFT+F5

Move Around in a Table

TASK	SHORTCUT
To the next cell in a row	TAB
To the previous cell in a row	SHIFT+TAB
To the first cell in a row	ALT+HOME
To the last cell in a row	ALT+END
To the first cell in a column	ALT+PAGE UP
To the last cell in a column	ALT+PAGE DOWN
To the previous row	UP ARROW
To the next row	DOWN ARROW

Row up	ALT+SHIFT+UP ARROW
Row down	ALT+SHIFT+DOWN ARROW

Insert paragraphs and tab characters in a table

TASK	SHORTCUT
New paragraphs in a cell	ENTER
Tab characters in a cell	CTRL+TAB

Use overtype mode

To change the overtype settings so that you can access overtype mode by pressing INSERT, do the following:

1. Press ALT+F, T to open **Word Options**.
2. Press A to select ADVANCED, and then press TAB.
3. Press ALT+O to move to the **Use the Insert key to control overtype mode** check box.
4. Press SPACEBAR to select the check box, and then press ENTER.

To turn Overtype mode on or off, press INSERT.

Character and paragraph formatting

Copy formatting

TASK	SHORTCUT
Copy formatting from text.	CTRL+SHIFT+C
Apply copied formatting to text.	CTRL+SHIFT+V

Change or resize the font

Note: The following keyboard shortcuts do not work in Full Screen Reading mode.

TASK	SHORTCUT
Open the **Font** dialog box to change the font.	CTRL+SHIFT+F
Increase the font size.	CTRL+SHIFT+>
Decrease the font size.	CTRL+SHIFT+<
Increase the font size by 1 point.	CTRL+]
Decrease the font size by 1 point.	CTRL+[

Apply character formats

TASK	SHORTCUT
Open the **Font** dialog box to change the formatting of characters.	CTRL+D
Change the case of letters.	SHIFT+F3
Format all letters as capitals.	CTRL+SHIFT+A
Apply bold formatting.	CTRL+B
Apply an underline.	CTRL+U
Underline words but not spaces.	CTRL+SHIFT+W
Double-underline text.	CTRL+SHIFT+D
Apply hidden text formatting.	CTRL+SHIFT+H
Apply italic formatting.	CTRL+I
Format letters as small capitals.	CTRL+SHIFT+K
Apply subscript formatting (automatic spacing).	CTRL+EQUAL SIGN
Apply superscript formatting (automatic spacing).	CTRL+SHIFT+PLUS SIGN
Remove manual character formatting.	CTRL+SPACEBAR
Change the selection to the Symbol font.	CTRL+SHIFT+Q

View and copy text formats

TASK	SHORTCUT
Display nonprinting characters.	CTRL+SHIFT+* (asterisk on numeric keypad does not work)
Review text formatting.	SHIFT+F1 (then click the text with the formatting you want to review)
Copy formats.	CTRL+SHIFT+C
Paste formats.	CTRL+SHIFT+V

Set the line spacing

TASK	SHORTCUT
Single-space lines.	CTRL+1
Double-space lines.	CTRL+2
Set 1.5-line spacing.	CTRL+5
Add or remove one line space preceding a paragraph.	CTRL+0 (zero)

Align paragraphs

TASK	SHORTCUT
Switch a paragraph between centered and left-aligned.	CTRL+E
Switch a paragraph between justified and left-aligned.	CTRL+J
Switch a paragraph between right-aligned and left-aligned.	CTRL+R
Left align a paragraph.	CTRL+L
Indent a paragraph from the left.	CTRL+M
Remove a paragraph indent from the left.	CTRL+SHIFT+M
Create a hanging indent.	CTRL+T
Reduce a hanging indent.	CTRL+SHIFT+T

| Remove paragraph formatting. | CTRL+Q |

Apply paragraph styles

TASK	SHORTCUT
Open **Apply Styles** task pane.	CTRL+SHIFT+S
Open **Styles** task pane.	ALT+CTRL+SHIFT+S
Start AutoFormat.	ALT+CTRL+K
Apply the Normal style.	CTRL+SHIFT+N
Apply the Heading 1 style.	ALT+CTRL+1
Apply the Heading 2 style.	ALT+CTRL+2
Apply the Heading 3 style.	ALT+CTRL+3

Close the Styles task pane

1. If the **Styles** task pane is not selected, press F6 to select it.
2. Press CTRL+SPACEBAR.
3. Use the arrow keys to select **Close**, and then press ENTER.

Insert and edit objects

Insert an object

1. Press ALT, N, J, and then J to open the **Object** dialog box.
2. Do one of the following.
   - Press DOWN ARROW to select an object type, and then press ENTER to create an object.
   - Press CTRL+TAB to switch to the **Create from File** tab, press TAB, and then type the file name of the object that you want to insert or browse to the file.

Edit an object

1. With the cursor positioned to the left of the object in your document, select the object by pressing SHIFT+RIGHT ARROW.
2. Press SHIFT+F10.
3. Press the TAB key to get to **Object name**, press ENTER, and then press ENTER again.

Insert SmartArt graphics

1. Press and release ALT, N, and then M to select **SmartArt**.
2. Press the arrow keys to select the type of graphic that you want.
3. Press TAB, and then press the arrow keys to select the graphic that you want to insert.
4. Press ENTER.

Insert WordArt

1. Press and release ALT, N, and then W to select **WordArt**.
2. Press the arrow keys to select the WordArt style that you want, and then press ENTER.
3. Type the text that you want.
4. Press ESC to select the WordArt object, and then use the arrow keys to move the object.
5. Press ESC again to return to return to the document.

Insert A SmartArt Graphic In An Office Document

1. In the Microsoft Office program where you want to insert the graphic, press Alt, then N, and then M to open the **SmartArt Graphic** dialog box.
2. Press Up Arrow or Down Arrow to select the type of graphic that you want.
3. Press Tab to move to the Layout task pane.
4. Press the arrow keys to select the layout that you want.
5. Press Enter to insert the selected layout.

Work With Shapes In A SmartArt Graphic.

TASK	SHORTCUT
Select the next element in a SmartArt graphic.	Tab
Select the previous element in a SmartArt graphic.	Shift+Tab
Select all shapes.	Ctrl +A
Remove focus from the selected shape.	Esc
Nudge the selected shape up.	Up Arrow
Nudge the selected shape down.	Down Arrow
Nudge the selected shape left.	Left Arrow
Nudge the selected shape right.	Right Arrow
Edit text in the selected shape.	Enter or F2, Esc to exit shape
Delete the selected shape.	Delete or Backspace
Cut the selected shape.	Ctrl+X or Shift+Delete
Copy the selected shape.	Ctrl+C
Paste the contents of the Clipboard.	Ctrl+V
Undo the last action.	Ctrl+Z

Move and resize shapes in a SmartArt graphic

TASK	SHORTCUT
Enlarge the selected shape horizontally.	Shift+Right Arrow
Reduce the selected shape horizontally.	Shift+Left Arrow
Enlarge the selected shape vertically.	Shift+Up Arrow
Reduce the selected shape vertically.	Shift+Down Arrow
Rotate the selected shape to the right.	Alt+Right Arrow
Rotate the selected shape to the left.	Alt+Left Arrow

Notes:

- To apply more precise adjustments to shapes, press the Ctrl key in addition to any of the above keyboard shortcuts.
- These keyboard shortcuts apply to multiple selections as if you selected each item individually.

Work With Text In A SmartArt Graphic

TASK	SHORTCUT
Move one character to the left.	Left Arrow
Move one character to the right.	Right Arrow
Move up one line.	Up Arrow
Move down one line.	Down Arrow
Move one word to the left.	Ctrl+Left Arrow
Move one word to the right.	Ctrl+Right Arrow
Move one paragraph up.	Ctrl+Up Arrow
Move one paragraph down.	Ctrl+Down Arrow
Move to the end of a line.	End

Move to the beginning of a line.	Home
Move to the end of a text box.	Ctrl+End
Move to the beginning of a text box.	Ctrl+Home
Cut selected text.	Ctrl+X
Copy selected text.	Ctrl+C
Paste selected text.	Ctrl+V
Move the selected text up.	Alt+Shift+Up Arrow
Move the selected text down.	Alt+Shift+Down Arrow
Undo the last action.	Ctrl+Z
Delete one character to the left.	Backspace
Delete one word to the left.	Ctrl+Backspace
Delete one character to the right.	Delete
Delete one word to the right.	Ctrl+Delete
Promote the selected text.	Alt+Shift+Left Arrow
Demote the selected text.	Alt+Shift+Right Arrow
Check the spelling (not available in Word).	F7

Apply character formatting

TASK	SHORTCUT
Open the **Font** dialog box.	Ctrl+Shift+F or Ctrl+Shift+P
Increase the font size of the selected text.	Ctrl+Shift+>
Decrease the font size of the selected text.	Ctrl+Shift+<
Switch the case of selected text (lower case, Title Case, UPPER CASE).	Shift+F3

Apply bold formatting to the selected text.	Ctrl+B
Apply an underline to the selected text.	Ctrl+U
Apply italic formatting to the selected text.	Ctrl+I
Apply subscript formatting to the selected text.	Ctrl+Equal Sign
Apply superscript formatting to the selected text.	Ctrl+Shift+Plus Sign
Adjust the superscript/subscript offset up.	Ctrl+Alt+Shift+>
Adjust the superscript/subscript offset down.	Ctrl+Alt+Shift+<
Remove all character formatting from the selected text.	Shift+Ctrl+Spacebar

Copy Text Formatting

TASK	SHORTCUT
Copy formatting from the selected text.	Shift+Ctrl+C
Paste formatting to the selected text.	Shift+Ctrl+V

Apply Paragraph Formatting

TASK	SHORTCUT
Center a paragraph.	Ctrl+E
Justify a paragraph.	Ctrl+J
Left align a paragraph.	Ctrl+L
Right align a paragraph.	Ctrl+R
Demote a bullet point.	Tab or Alt+Shift+Right Arrow

| Promote a bullet point. | Shift+Tab or Alt+Shift+Left Arrow |

Use The Text Pane

TASK	SHORTCUT
Merge two lines of text.	Delete at the end of the first line of text
Display the shortcut menu.	Shift+F10
Switch between the **Text** pane and the drawing canvas.	Ctrl+Shift+F2
Close the **Text** pane.	Alt+F4
Switch the focus from the **Text** pane to the border of the SmartArt graphic.	Esc
Open the SmartArt graphics Help topic. (Your pointer should be in the Text pane.)	Ctrl +Shift+F1

Mail merge and fields

Perform a mail merge

Note: You must be on the **Mailings** tab to use these keyboard shortcuts.

TASK	SHORTCUT
Preview a mail merge.	ALT+SHIFT+K
Merge a document.	ALT+SHIFT+N
Print the merged document.	ALT+SHIFT+M
Edit a mail-merge data document.	ALT+SHIFT+E
Insert a merge field.	ALT+SHIFT+F

Work with fields

TASK	SHORTCUT
Insert a DATE field.	ALT+SHIFT+D
Insert a LISTNUM field.	ALT+CTRL+L
Insert a PAGE field.	ALT+SHIFT+P
Insert a TIME field.	ALT+SHIFT+T
Insert an empty field.	CTRL+F9
Update linked information in a Microsoft Word source document.	CTRL+SHIFT+F7
Update selected fields.	F9
Unlink a field.	CTRL+SHIFT+F9
Switch between a selected field code and its result.	SHIFT+F9
Switch between all field codes and their results.	ALT+F9
Run GOTOBUTTON or MACROBUTTON from the field that displays the field results.	ALT+SHIFT+F9
Go to the next field.	F11
Go to the previous field.	SHIFT+F11
Lock a field.	CTRL+F11
Unlock a field.	CTRL+SHIFT+F11

Language Bar

Handwriting recognition

TASK	SHORTCUT
Switch between languages or keyboard layouts.	Left ALT+SHIFT
Display a list of correction alternatives.	+C
Turn handwriting on or off.	+H

Turn Japanese Input Method Editor (IME) on 101 keyboard on or off.	ALT+~
Turn Korean IME on 101 keyboard on or off.	Right ALT
Turn Chinese IME on 101 keyboard on or off.	CTRL+SPACEBAR

Tips

- You can choose the key combination for switching between languages or keyboard layouts in the **Advanced Key Setting** dialog box. To open the **Advanced Key Setting** dialog box, right-click the **Language** bar, and then click **Settings**. Under **Preferences**, click **Key Settings**.
- The Windows logo key is available on the bottom row of keys on most keyboards.

Function Key Reference.

Function Keys

TASK	SHORTCUT
Get Help or visit Microsoft Office.com.	F1
Move text or graphics.	F2
Repeat the last action.	F4
Choose the **Go To** command (**Home** tab).	F5
Go to the next pane or frame.	F6
Choose the **Spelling** command (**Review** tab).	F7
Extend a selection.	F8
Update the selected fields.	F9

Show KeyTips.	F10
Go to the next field.	F11
Choose the **Save As** command.	F12

SHIFT+Function Key

TASK	SHORTCUT
Start context-sensitive Help or reveal formatting.	SHIFT+F1
Copy text.	SHIFT+F2
Change the case of letters.	SHIFT+F3
Repeat a **Find** or **Go To** action.	SHIFT+F4
Move to the last change.	SHIFT+F5
Go to the previous pane or frame (after pressing F6).	SHIFT+F6
Choose the **Thesaurus** command (**Review** tab, **Proofing** group).	SHIFT+F7
Reduce the size of a selection.	SHIFT+F8
Switch between a field code and its result.	SHIFT+F9
Display a shortcut menu.	SHIFT+F10
Go to the previous field.	SHIFT+F11
Choose the **Save** command.	SHIFT+F12

CTRL+Function Key

TASK	SHORTCUT
Expand or collapse the Ribbon.	CTRL+F1
Choose the **Print Preview** command.	CTRL+F2
Cut to the Spike.	CTRL+F3
Close the window.	CTRL+F4
Go to the next window.	CTRL+F6
Insert an empty field.	CTRL+F9
Maximize the document window.	CTRL+F10

Lock a field.	CTRL+F11
Choose the **Open** command.	CTRL+F12

CTRL+SHIFT+Function Key

TASK	SHORTCUT
Insert the contents of the Spike.	CTRL+SHIFT+F3
Edit a bookmark.	CTRL+SHIFT+F5
Go to the previous window.	CTRL+SHIFT+F6
Update linked information in an Word 2010 source document.	CTRL+SHIFT+F7
Extend a selection or block.	CTRL+SHIFT+F8, and then press an arrow key
Unlink a field.	CTRL+SHIFT+F9
Unlock a field.	CTRL+SHIFT+F11
Choose the **Print** command.	CTRL+SHIFT+F12

ALT+Function Key

TASK	SHORTCUT
Go to the next field.	ALT+F1
Create a new **Building Block**.	ALT+F3
Exit Word 2010.	ALT+F4
Restore the program window size.	ALT+F5
Move from an open dialog box back to the document, for dialog boxes that support this behavior.	ALT+F6
Find the next misspelling or grammatical error.	ALT+F7
Run a macro.	ALT+F8

Switch between all field codes and their results.	ALT+F9
Display the **Selection and Visibility** task pane.	ALT+F10
Display Microsoft Visual Basic code.	ALT+F11

ALT+SHIFT+Function Key

TASK	SHORTCUT
Go to the previous field.	ALT+SHIFT+F1
Choose the **Save** command.	ALT+SHIFT+F2
Display the **Research** task pane.	ALT+SHIFT+F7
Run GOTOBUTTON or MACROBUTTON from the field that displays the field results.	ALT+SHIFT+F9
Display a menu or message for an available action.	ALT+SHIFT+F10
Choose **Table of Contents** button in the Table of Contents container when the container is active.	ALT+SHIFT+F12

CTRL+ALT+Function Key

TASK	SHORTCUT
Display Microsoft System Information.	CTRL+ALT+F1
Choose the **Open** command.	CTRL+ALT+F2

Note: If you are using Microsoft Word Starter, be aware that not all the features listed for Word are supported in Word Starter. For more information about the features available in Word Starter.

CHAPTER 5

Keyboard Shortcuts For Use In Outlook 2010.

Definition of Program: Microsoft Outlook is a program designed by Microsoft Corporation that keeps people connected through its email services with powerful organizational tools.

The following keyboard shortcuts will help you become a successful user of Microsoft Outlook 2010.

Common Procedure.

Basic Navigation

TASK	SHORTCUT
Switch to Mail.	CTRL+1
Switch to Calendar.	CTRL+2
Switch to Contacts.	CTRL+3
Switch to Tasks.	CTRL+4
Switch to Notes.	CTRL+5
Switch to Folder List in **Navigation Pane**.	CTRL+6
Switch to Shortcuts.	CTRL+7
Switch to next message (with message open).	CTRL+PERIOD
Switch to previous message (with message open).	CTRL+COMMA
Move between the **Navigation Pane**, the main	CTRL+SHIFT+TAB or SHIFT+TAB

Outlook window, the **Reading Pane**, and the **To-Do Bar**.	
Move between the Outlook window, the smaller panes in the **Navigation Pane**, the **Reading Pane**, and the sections in the **To-Do Bar**.	TAB
Move between the Outlook window, the smaller panes in the **Navigation Pane**, the **Reading Pane**, and the sections in the **To-Do Bar**, and show the access keys in the Outlook ribbon.	F6
Move around message header lines in the **Navigation Pane** or an open message.	CTRL+TAB
Move around within the **Navigation Pane**.	Arrow keys
Go to a different folder.	CTRL+Y
Go to the **Search** box.	F3 or CTRL+E
In the **Reading Pane**, go to the previous message.	ALT+UP ARROW or CTRL+COMMA or ALT+PAGE UP
In the **Reading Pane**, page down through text.	SPACEBAR
In the **Reading Pane**, page up through text.	SHIFT+SPACEBAR
Collapse or expand a group in the email message list.	LEFT ARROW or RIGHT ARROW
Go back to previous view in main Outlook window.	ALT+B or ALT+LEFT ARROW
Go forward to next view in main Outlook window.	ALT+RIGHT ARROW

Select the **InfoBar** and, if available, show the menu of commands.	CTRL+SHIFT+W

Search

TASK	SHORTCUT
Find a message or other item.	CTRL+E
Clear the search results.	ESC
Expand the search to include **All Mail Items**, **All Calendar Items**, or **All Contact Items**, depending on the view that you are in.	CTRL+ALT+A
Use **Advanced Find**.	CTRL+SHIFT+F
Create a Search Folder.	CTRL+SHIFT+P
Search for text inside an open item.	F4
Find and replace text, symbols, or some formatting commands. Works in the **Reading Pane** on an open item.	CTRL+H
Expand search to include items from the current folder.	CTRL+ALT+K
Expand search to include subfolders.	CTRL+ALT+Z

Flags

TASK	SHORTCUT
Open the **Flag for Follow Up** dialog box to assign a flag.	CTRL+SHIFT+G

Color Categories

TASK	SHORTCUT
Delete the selected category from the list in the **Color Categories** dialog box.	ALT+D

Create An Item or File

TASK	SHORTCUT
Create an appointment.	CTRL+SHIFT+A
Create a contact.	CTRL+SHIFT+C
Create a Contact List.	CTRL+SHIFT+L
Create a fax.	CTRL+SHIFT+X
Create a folder.	CTRL+SHIFT+E
Create a Journal entry.	CTRL+SHIFT+J
Create a meeting request.	CTRL+SHIFT+Q
Create a message.	CTRL+SHIFT+M
Create a note.	CTRL+SHIFT+N
Create a Microsoft Office document.	CTRL+SHIFT+H
Post to this folder.	CTRL+SHIFT+S
Post a reply in this folder.	CTRL+T
Create a Search Folder.	CTRL+SHIFT+P
Create a task.	CTRL+SHIFT+K
Create a task request.	CTRL+SHIFT+U

Procedures in all items

TASK	SHORTCUT
Save (except in Tasks).	CTRL+S or SHIFT+F12
Save and close (except in Mail).	ALT+S
Save as (only in Mail).	F12
Undo.	CTRL+Z or ALT+BACKSPACE

Delete an item.	CTRL+D
Print.	CTRL+P
Copy an item.	CTRL+SHIFT+Y
Move an item.	CTRL+SHIFT+V
Check names.	CTRL+K
Check spelling.	F7
Flag for follow-up.	CTRL+SHIFT+G
Forward.	CTRL+F
Send or post or invite all.	ALT+S
Enable editing in a field (except in Mail or Icon view).	F2
Left align text.	CTRL+L
Center text.	CTRL+E
Right align text.	CTRL+R

Email

TASK	SHORTCUT
Switch to **Inbox**.	CTRL+SHIFT+I
Switch to **Outbox**.	CTRL+SHIFT+O
Choose the account from which to send a message.	CTRL+TAB (with the focus on the **To** box), and then TAB to the **Accounts** button
Check names.	CTRL+K
Send.	ALT+S
Reply to a message.	CTRL+R
Reply all to a message.	CTRL+SHIFT+R
Reply with meeting request.	CTRL+ALT+R
Forward a message.	CTRL+F
Mark a message as not junk.	CTRL+ ALT+J

Display blocked external content (in a message).	CTRL+SHIFT+I
Post to a folder.	CTRL+ SHIFT+S
Apply Normal style.	CTRL+SHIFT+N
Check for new messages.	CTRL+M or F9
Go to the previous message.	UP ARROW
Go to the next message.	DOWN ARROW
Create a message (when in Mail).	CTRL+N
Create a message (from any Outlook view).	CTRL+SHIFT+M
Open a received message.	CTRL+O
Delete and Ignore a Conversation.	CTRL+DELETE
Open the Address Book.	CTRL+SHIFT+B
Add a Quick Flag to an unopened message.	INSERT
Display the **Flag for Follow Up** dialog box.	CTRL+SHIFT+G
Mark as read.	CTRL+Q
Mark as unread.	CTRL+U
Open the Mail Tip in the selected message.	CTRL+SHIFT+W
Find or replace.	F4
Find next.	SHIFT+F4
Send.	CTRL+ENTER

Print.	CTRL+P
Forward.	CTRL+F
Forward as attachment.	CTRL+ALT+F
Show the properties for the selected item.	ALT+ENTER
Create a multimedia message	CTRL+SHIFT+U
Create a text message.	CTRL+SHIFT+T
Mark for Download.	CTRL+ALT+M
Clear Mark for Download.	CTRL+ALT+U
Display Send/Receive progress.	CTRL+B (when a Send/Receive is in progress)

Calendar

TASK	SHORTCUT
Create an appointment (when in Calendar).	CTRL+N
Create an appointment (in any Outlook view).	CTRL+SHIFT+A
Create a meeting request.	CTRL+SHIFT+Q
Forward an appointment or meeting.	CTRL+F
Reply to a meeting request with a message.	CTRL+R
Reply All to a meeting request with a message.	CTRL+SHIFT+R
Show 10 days in the calendar.	ALT+0
Show 1 day in the calendar.	ALT+1

Show 2 days in the calendar.	ALT+2
Show 3 days in the calendar.	ALT+3
Show 4 days in the calendar.	ALT+4
Show 5 days in the calendar.	ALT+5
Show 6 days in the calendar.	ALT+6
Show 7 days in the calendar.	ALT+7
Show 8 days in the calendar.	ALT+8
Show 9 days in the calendar.	ALT+9
Go to a date.	CTRL+G
Switch to Month view.	ALT+= or CTRL+ALT+4
Go to the next day.	CTRL+RIGHT ARROW
Go to the next week.	ALT+DOWN ARROW
Go to the next month.	ALT+PAGE DOWN
Go to the previous day.	CTRL+LEFT ARROW
Go to the previous week.	ALT+UP ARROW
Go to the previous month.	ALT+PAGE UP
Go to the start of the week.	ALT+HOME
Go to the end of the week.	ALT+END
Switch to Full Week view.	ALT+MINUS SIGN or CTRL+ALT+3
Switch to Work Week view.	CTRL+ALT+2

Go to previous appointment.	CTRL+COMMA or CTRL+SHIFT+COMMA
Go to next appointment.	CTRL+PERIOD or CTRL+SHIFT+PERIOD
Set up recurrence for an open appointment or meeting.	CTRL+G

See also under Views, Calendar Day/Week/Month view, and Date Navigator

Contacts

TASK	SHORTCUT
Dial a new call.	CTRL+SHIFT+D
Find a contact or other item (Search).	F3 or CTRL+E
Enter a name in the **Search Address Books** box.	F11
In the Card or Business Card view of contacts, go to the first contact that begins with a specific letter.	SHIFT+letter
Select all contacts.	CTRL+A
Create a message that uses the selected contact as subject.	CTRL+F
Create a Journal entry for the selected contact.	CTRL+J
Create a contact (when in Contacts).	CTRL+N
Create a contact (from any Outlook view).	CTRL+SHIFT+C
Open a contact form that uses the selected contact.	CTRL+O

Create a Contact List.	CTRL+SHIFT+L
Print.	CTRL+P
Update a list of Contact List members.	F5
Go to a different folder.	CTRL+Y
Open the Address Book.	CTRL+SHIFT+B
Use **Advanced Find**.	CTRL+SHIFT+F
In an open contact, open the next contact listed.	CTRL+SHIFT+PERIOD
Find a contact.	F11
Close a contact.	ESC
Send a fax to the selected contact.	CTRL+SHIFT+X
Open the **Check Address** dialog box.	ALT+D
In a contact form, under **Internet**, display the **E-mail 1** information.	ALT+SHIFT+1
In a contact form, under **Internet**, display the **E-mail 2** information.	ALT+SHIFT+2
In a contact form, under **Internet**, display the **E-mail 3** information.	ALT+SHIFT+3

In the Electronic Business Cards dialog box

TASK	SHORTCUT
Open the **Add** list.	ALT+A
Select text in **Label** box when the field that has a label assigned is selected.	ALT+B
Open the **Add Card Picture** dialog box.	ALT+C

Place the cursor at beginning of **Edit** box.	ALT+E
Select the **Fields** box.	ALT+F
Select the **Image Align** drop-down list.	ALT+G
Select color palette for background.	ALT+K, then ENTER
Select **Layout** drop-down list.	ALT+L
Remove a selected field from the **Fields** box.	ALT+R

Tasks

TASK	SHORTCUT
Show or hide the **To-Do Bar**.	ALT+F2
Accept a task request.	ALT+C
Decline a task request.	ALT+D
Find a task or other item.	CTRL+E
Open the **Go to Folder** dialog box.	CTRL+Y
Create a task (when in Tasks).	CTRL+N
Create a task (from any Outlook view).	CTRL+SHIFT+K
Open selected item.	CTRL+O
Print selected item.	CTRL+P
Select all items.	CTRL+A
Delete selected item.	CTRL+D
Forward a task as an attachment.	CTRL+F
Create a task request.	CTRL+SHIFT+ALT+U
Switch between the **Navigation Pane**, **Tasks** list, and **To-Do Bar**.	TAB or SHIFT+TAB

Open selected item as a Journal item.	CTRL+J
Undo last action.	CTRL+Z
Flag an item or mark complete.	INSERT

Format Text

TASK	SHORTCUT
Display the **Format** menu.	ALT+O
Display the **Font** dialog box.	CTRL+SHIFT+P
Switch case (with text selected).	SHIFT+F3
Format letters as small capitals.	CTRL+SHIFT+K
Make letters bold.	CTRL+B
Add bullets.	CTRL+SHIFT+L
Make letters italic.	CTRL+I
Increase indent.	CTRL+T
Decrease indent.	CTRL+SHIFT+T
Left align.	CTRL+L
Center.	CTRL+E
Underline.	CTRL+U
Increase font size.	CTRL+] or CTRL+SHIFT+>
Decrease font size.	CTRL+[or CTRL+SHIFT+<
Cut.	CTRL+X or SHIFT+DELETE
Copy.	CTRL+C or CTRL+INSERT **Note:** CTRL+INSERT isn't available in the Reading Pane.
Paste.	CTRL+V or SHIFT+INSERT
Clear formatting.	CTRL+SHIFT+Z or CTRL+SPACEBAR

Delete the next word.	CTRL+SHIFT+H
Stretch a paragraph to fit between the margins.	CTRL+SHIFT+J
Apply styles.	CTRL+SHIFT+S
Create a hanging indent.	CTRL+T
Insert a hyperlink.	CTRL+K
Left align a paragraph.	CTRL+L
Right align a paragraph.	CTRL+R
Reduce a hanging indent.	CTRL+SHIFT+T
Remove paragraph formatting.	CTRL+Q

Add Web Information To Items

TASK	SHORTCUT
Edit a URL in the body of an item.	Hold down CTRL and then click.
Insert a hyperlink.	CTRL+K

Printing

TASK	SHORTCUT
Open **Print** tab in Backstage view.	Press ALT+F, and then press P
To print an item from an open window.	ALT+F, press P, and then press F and press 1
Open **Page Setup** from **Print Preview**.	ALT+S or ALT+U

To select a printer from **Print Preview**.	ALT+F, press P, and then press I
To **Define Print Styles**.	ALT+F, press P, and then press L
To open **Print Options**.	ALT+F, press P, and then press R

Send/Receive

TASK	SHORTCUT
Start a send/receive for all defined Send/Receive groups with **Include this group in Send/Receive (F9)** selected. This can include headers, full items, specified folders, items less than a specific size, or any combination that you define.	F9
Start a send/receive for the current folder, retrieving full items (header, item, and any attachments).	SHIFT+F9
Start a send/receive.	CTRL+M
Define Send/Receive groups.	CTRL+ALT+S

Visual Basic Editor

TASK	SHORTCUT
Open Visual Basic Editor.	ALT+F11

Macros

TASK	SHORTCUT
Play macro.	ALT+F8

Forms

TASK	SHORTCUT
Create an Office InfoPath form.	Click in an InfoPath folder, and then CTRL+N.
Choose an Microsoft InfoPath form.	CTRL+SHIFT+ALT+T

Views

Table View

General Use

TASK	SHORTCUT
Open an item.	ENTER
Select all items.	CTRL+A
Go to the item at the bottom of the screen.	PAGE DOWN
Go to the item at the top of the screen.	PAGE UP
Extend or reduce the selected items by one item.	SHIFT+UP ARROW or SHIFT+DOWN ARROW, respectively
Go to the next or previous item without extending the selection.	CTRL+UP ARROW or CTRL+DOWN ARROW, respectively
Select or cancel selection of the active item.	CTRL+SPACEBAR

With a Group Selected

TASK	SHORTCUT
Expand a single selected group.	RIGHT ARROW
Collapse a single selected group.	LEFT ARROW
Select the previous group.	UP ARROW
Select the next group.	DOWN ARROW
Select the first group.	HOME
Select the last group.	END
Select the first item on screen in an expanded group or the first item off screen to the right.	RIGHT ARROW

Calendar Day/Week/Month View

All three

TASK	SHORTCUT
View from 1 through 9 days.	ALT+key for number of days
View 10 days.	ALT+0 (ZERO)
Switch to weeks.	ALT+MINUS SIGN
Switch to months.	ALT+=
Move between **Calendar**, **TaskPad**, and the **Folder List**.	CTRL+TAB or F6
Select the previous appointment.	SHIFT+TAB
Go to the previous day.	LEFT ARROW
Go to the next day.	RIGHT ARROW
Go to the same day in the next week.	ALT+DOWN ARROW
Go to the same day in the previous week.	ALT+UP ARROW

Day view

TASK	SHORTCUT
Select the time that begins your work day.	HOME
Select the time that ends your work day.	END
Select the previous block of time.	UP ARROW
Select the next block of time.	DOWN ARROW
Select the block of time at the top of the screen.	PAGE UP
Select the block of time at the bottom of the screen.	PAGE DOWN
Extend or reduce the selected time.	SHIFT+UP ARROW or SHIFT+DOWN ARROW
Move an appointment up or down.	With the cursor in the appointment, ALT+UP ARROW or ALT+DOWN ARROW
Change an appointment's start or end time.	With the cursor in the appointment, ALT+SHIFT+UP ARROW or ALT+SHIFT+DOWN ARROW
Move selected item to the same day in the next week.	ALT+DOWN ARROW
Move selected item to the same day in the previous week.	ALT+UP ARROW

Week View

TASK	SHORTCUT
Go to the start of work hours for the selected day.	HOME
Go to the end of work hours for the selected day.	END
Go up one page view in the selected day.	PAGE UP
Go down one page view in the selected day.	PAGE DOWN
Change the duration of the selected block of time.	SHIFT+LEFT ARROW, SHIFT+RIGHT ARROW, SHIFT+UP ARROW, or SHIFT+DOWN ARROW; or SHIFT+HOME or SHIFT+END

Month View

TASK	SHORTCUT
Go to the first day of the week.	HOME
Go to the same day of the week in the previous page.	PAGE UP
Go to the same day of the week in the next page.	PAGE DOWN

Date Navigator

TASK	SHORTCUT
Go to the first day of the current week.	ALT+HOME

Go to the last day of the current week.	ALT+END
Go to the same day in the previous week.	ALT+UP ARROW
Go to the same day in the next week.	ALT+DOWN ARROW

Business Cards View or Address Cards View

General Use

TASK	SHORTCUT
Select a specific card in the list.	One or more letters of the name that the card is filed under or the name of the field that you are sorting by
Select the previous card.	UP ARROW
Select the next card.	DOWN ARROW
Select the first card in the list.	HOME
Select the last card in the list.	END
Select the first card on the current page.	PAGE UP
Select the first card on the next page.	PAGE DOWN
Select the closest card in the next column.	RIGHT ARROW
Select the closest card in the previous column.	LEFT ARROW

Select or cancel selection of the active card.	CTRL+SPACEBAR
Extend the selection to the previous card and cancel selection of cards after the starting point.	SHIFT+UP ARROW
Extend the selection to the next card and cancel selection of cards before the starting point.	SHIFT+DOWN ARROW
Extend the selection to the previous card, regardless of the starting point.	CTRL+SHIFT+UP ARROW
Extend the selection to the next card, regardless of the starting point.	CTRL+SHIFT+DOWN ARROW
Extend the selection to the first card in the list.	SHIFT+HOME
Extend the selection to the last card in the list.	SHIFT+END
Extend the selection to the first card on the previous page.	SHIFT+PAGE UP
Extend the selection to the last card on the last page.	SHIFT+PAGE DOWN

Move Between Fields In An Open Card.

To use the following keys, make sure a field in a card is selected. To select a field when a card is selected, click the field.

TASK	SHORTCUT
Move to the next field and control.	TAB
Move to the previous field and, control.	SHIFT+TAB
Close the active card.	ENTER

Move Between Characters in a Field

To use the following keys, make sure a field in a card is selected. To select a field when a card is selected, click the field.

TASK	SHORTCUT
Add a line in a multiline field.	ENTER
Move to the beginning of a line.	HOME
Move to the end of a line.	END
Move to the beginning of a multiline field.	PAGE UP
Move to the end of a multiline field.	PAGE DOWN
Move to the previous line in a multiline field.	UP ARROW
Move to the next line in a multiline field.	DOWN ARROW
Move to the previous character in a field.	LEFT ARROW
Move to the next character in a field.	RIGHT ARROW

Timeline View (Tasks or Journal)

When an item is selected

TASK	SHORTCUT
Select the previous item.	LEFT ARROW
Select the next item.	RIGHT ARROW
Select several adjacent items.	SHIFT+LEFT ARROW or SHIFT+RIGHT ARROW
Select several nonadjacent items.	CTRL+LEFT ARROW+SPACEBAR or CTRL+RIGHT ARROW+SPACEBAR
Open the selected items.	ENTER
Select the first item on the timeline (if items aren't grouped) or the first item in the group.	HOME
Select the last item on the timeline (if items aren't grouped) or the last item in the group.	END
Display (without selecting) the first item on the timeline (if items aren't grouped) or the first item in the group.	CTRL+HOME
Display (without selecting) the last item on the timeline (if items aren't grouped) or the last item in the group.	CTRL+END

When a Group is Selected

TASK	SHORTCUT
Expand the group.	ENTER or RIGHT ARROW
Collapse the group.	ENTER or LEFT ARROW
Select the previous group.	UP ARROW
Select the next group.	DOWN ARROW
Select the first group on the timeline.	HOME
Select the last group on the timeline.	END
Select the first item on screen in an expanded group or the first item off screen to the right.	RIGHT ARROW

When a unit of time on the time scale for days is selected

TASK	SHORTCUT
Move back in increments of time that are the same as those shown on the time scale.	LEFT ARROW
Move forward in increments of time that are the same as those shown on the time scale.	RIGHT ARROW
Switch between active view, To-Do Bar, Search, Journal folders and back to active view.	TAB and SHIFT+TAB

Note: Some of the contents of this topic may not be applicable to some languages.

CHAPTER 6

Keyboard Shortcuts For Use In OneNote 2010.

Definition of Program: Microsoft OneNote is a Program designed by Microsoft Corporation in the year 2003 that is used for note-taking.

Note: Some of the content in this topic may not be applicable to some languages.

The following keyboard shortcuts will help you become a successful user of Microsoft OneNote 2010.

Taking And Formatting Notes

Typing and Editing Notes

TASK	SHORTCUT
Open a new OneNote window.	CTRL+M
Open a small OneNote window to create a side note.	CTRL+SHIFT+M
Dock the OneNote window.	CTRL+ALT+D
Undo the last action.	CTRL+Z
Redo the last action.	CTRL+Y
Select all items on the current page.	CTRL+A

Note: Press CTRL+A more than once to increase the scope of the selection.	
Cut the selected text or item.	CTRL+X
Copy the selected text or item to the Clipboard.	CTRL+C
Paste the contents of the Clipboard.	CTRL+V
Move to the beginning of the line.	HOME
Move to the end of the line.	END
Move one character to the left.	LEFT ARROW
Move one character to the right.	RIGHT ARROW
Move one word to the left.	CTRL+LEFT ARROW
Move one word to the right.	CTRL+RIGHT ARROW
Delete one character to the left.	BACKSPACE
Delete one character to the right.	DELETE
Delete one word to the left.	CTRL+BACKSPACE
Delete one word to the right.	CTRL+DELETE
Insert a line break without starting a new paragraph.	SHIFT+ENTER
Check spelling.	F7
Open the thesaurus for the currently selected word.	SHIFT+F7
Bring up the context menu for any note, tab, or any other object that currently has focus.	SHIFT+F10
Execute the action suggested on the Information Bar if it appears at the top of a page.	CTRL+SHIFT+W

Formatting Notes

TASK	SHORTCUT
Highlight selected text in yellow.	CTRL+SHIFT+H or CTRL+ALT+H
Insert a hyperlink.	CTRL+K
Copy the formatting of selected text (Format Painter).	CTRL+SHIFT+C
Paste the formatting to selected text (Format Painter).	CTRL+SHIFT+V
Open a hyperlink. **Note:** The cursor must be placed anywhere within the formatted hyperlink text.	ENTER
Apply or remove bold formatting from the selected text.	CTRL+B
Apply or remove italic formatting from the selected text.	CTRL+I
Apply or remove the underline from the selected text.	CTRL+U
Apply or remove strikethrough from the selected text.	CTRL+HYPHEN
Apply or remove superscript formatting from the selected text.	CTRL+SHIFT+=
Apply or remove subscript formatting from the selected text.	CTRL+=
Apply or remove bulleted list formatting from the selected paragraph.	CTRL+PERIOD

Apply or remove numbered list formatting from the selected paragraph.	CTRL+SLASH
Apply a Heading 1 style to the current note.	CTRL+ALT+1
Apply a Heading 2 style to the current note.	CTRL+ALT+2
Apply a Heading 3 style to the current note.	CTRL+ALT+3
Apply a Heading 4 style to the current note.	CTRL+ALT+4
Apply a Heading 5 style to the current note.	CTRL+ALT+5
Apply a Heading 6 style to the current note.	CTRL+ALT+6
Apply the Normal style to the current note.	CTRL+SHIFT+N
Indent a paragraph from the left.	ALT+SHIFT+RIGHT ARROW
Remove a paragraph indent from the left.	ALT+SHIFT+LEFT ARROW
RIGHT-ALIGN THE SELECTED PARAGRAPH.	CTRL+R
Left-align the selected paragraph.	CTRL+L
Increase the font size of selected text.	CTRL+SHIFT+>
Decrease the font size of selected text.	CTRL+SHIFT+<
Clear all formatting applied to the selected text.	CTRL+SHIFT+N
Show or hide rule lines on the current page.	CTRL+SHIFT+R

Adding Items to a Page

TASK	SHORTCUT
Insert a document or file on the current page.	ALT+N, F
Insert a document or file as a printout on the current page.	ALT+N, O
Show or hide document printouts on the current page (when running OneNote in High Contrast mode).	ALT+SHIFT+P
Insert a picture from a file.	ALT+N, P
Insert a picture from a scanner or a camera.	ALT+N, S
Insert a screen clipping. **Note:** The OneNote icon must be active in the notification area, at the far right of the Windows taskbar.	Windows logo key+S
Insert the current date.	ALT+SHIFT+D
Insert the current date and time.	ALT+SHIFT+F
Insert the current time.	ALT+SHIFT+T
Insert a line break.	SHIFT+ENTER
Start a math equation or convert selected text to a math equation.	ALT+=
Create a table by adding a second column to already typed text.	TAB
Create another column in a table with a single row.	TAB
Create another row when at the end cell of a table. **Note:** Press ENTER a second time to finish the table.	ENTER
Create a row below the current row in a table.	CTRL+ENTER

Create another paragraph in the same cell in a table.	ALT+ENTER
Create a column to the right of the current column in a table.	CTRL+ALT+R
Create a column to the left of the current column in a table.	CTRL+ALT+E
Create a row above the current one in a table (when the cursor is at the beginning of any row).	ENTER
Delete the current empty row in a table (when the cursor is at the beginning of the row).	DEL (press twice)

Selecting Notes and Objects

TASK	SHORTCUT
Select all items on the current page. **Note:** Press CTRL+A more than once to increase the scope of the selection.	CTRL+A
Select to the end of the line.	SHIFT+END
Select the whole line (when the cursor is at the beginning of the line).	SHIFT+DOWN ARROW
Jump to the title of the page and select it.	CTRL+SHIFT+T
Cancel the selected outline or page.	ESC
Move the current paragraph or several selected paragraphs up.	ALT+SHIFT+UP ARROW

Move the current paragraph or several selected paragraphs down.	ALT+SHIFT+DOWN ARROW
Move the current paragraph or several selected paragraphs left (decreasing the indent).	ALT+SHIFT+LEFT ARROW
Move the current paragraph or several selected paragraphs right (increasing the indent).	ALT+SHIFT+RIGHT ARROW
Select the current paragraph and its subordinate paragraphs.	CTRL+SHIFT+HYPHEN
Delete the selected note or object.	DELETE
Move to the beginning of the line.	HOME
Move to the end of the line.	END
Move one character to the left.	LEFT ARROW
Move one character to the right.	RIGHT ARROW
Go back to the last page visited.	ALT+LEFT ARROW
Go forward to the next page visited.	ALT+RIGHT ARROW
Start playback of a selected audio or video recording.	CTRL+ALT+P
Start playback of a selected audio or video recording.	CTRL+ALT+S
Rewind the current audio or video recording by a few seconds.	CTRL+ALT+Y

Fast-forward the current audio or video recording by a few seconds.	CTRL+ALT+U

Tagging Notes

TASK	SHORTCUT
Apply, mark, or clear the To Do tag.	CTRL+1
Apply or clear the Important tag.	CTRL+2
Apply or clear the Question tag.	CTRL+3
Apply or clear the Remember for later tag.	CTRL+4
Apply or clear the Definition tag.	CTRL+5
Apply or clear a custom tag.	CTRL+6
Apply or clear a custom tag.	CTRL+7
Apply or clear a custom tag.	CTRL+8
Apply or clear a custom tag.	CTRL+9
Remove all note tags from the selected notes.	CTRL+0

Using Outlines

TASK	SHORTCUT
Show through Level 1.	ALT+SHIFT+1
Expand to Level 2.	ALT+SHIFT+2
Expand to Level 3.	ALT+SHIFT+3
Expand to Level 4.	ALT+SHIFT+4
Expand to Level 5.	ALT+SHIFT+5
Expand to Level 6.	ALT+SHIFT+6
Expand to Level 7.	ALT+SHIFT+7
Expand to Level 8.	ALT+SHIFT+8
Expand to Level 9.	ALT+SHIFT+9
Expand all levels.	ALT+SHIFT+0

Increase indent by one level.	TAB
Decrease indent by one level.	SHIFT+TAB
Expand a collapsed outline.	ALT+SHIFT+PLUS SIGN
Collapse an expanded outline.	ALT+SHIFT+MINUS SIGN

Specifying Language Settings

Note: To change the writing direction for your notes, you must first enable right-to-left languages in the **Microsoft Office 2010 Language Preferences** tool.

TASK	SHORTCUT
Set writing direction left to right.	CTRL+LEFT SHIFT
Set writing direction right to left.	CTRL+RIGHT SHIFT
Increase indent by one level in right-to-left text.	TAB
Decrease indent by one level in right-to-left text.	SHIFT+TAB

Organizing And Managing Your Notebook.

Working with pages and side notes

TASK	SHORTCUT
Enable or disable full page view.	F11
Open a new OneNote window.	CTRL+M

Open a small OneNote window to create a side note.	CTRL+SHIFT+M
Expand or collapse the tabs of a page group.	CTRL+SHIFT+*
Print the current page.	CTRL+P
Add a new page at the end of the selected section.	CTRL+N
Increase the width of the page tabs bar.	CTRL+SHIFT+[
Decrease the width of the page tabs bar.	CTRL+SHIFT+]
Create a new page below the current page tab at the same level.	CTRL+ALT+N
Decrease indent level of the current page tab label.	CTRL+ALT+[
Increase indent level of the current page tab label.	CTRL+ALT+]
Create a new subpage below the current page.	CTRL+SHIFT+ALT+N
Select all items. **Note:** Press CTRL+A several times to increase the scope of the selection.	CTRL+A

Select the current page.	CTRL+SHIFT+A If the selected page is part of a group, press CTRL+A to select all of the pages in the group.
Move the selected page tab up.	ALT+SHIFT+UP ARROW
Move the selected page tab down.	ALT+SHIFT+DOWN ARROW
Move the insertion point to the page title.	CTRL+SHIFT+T
Go to the first page in the currently visible set of page tabs.	ALT+PAGE UP
Go to the last page in the currently visible set of page tabs.	ALT+PAGE DOWN
Scroll up in the current page.	PAGE UP
Scroll down in the current page.	PAGE DOWN
Scroll to the top of the current page.	CTRL+HOME
Scroll to the bottom of the current page.	CTRL+END
Go to the next paragraph.	CTRL+DOWN ARROW
Go to the previous paragraph.	CTRL+UP ARROW
Move the insertion point up in the	CTRL+ALT+UP ARROW

current page, or expand the page up.	
Move the insertion point down in the current page, or expand the page down.	CTRL+ALT+DOWN ARROW
Move the insertion point left in the current page, or expand the page to the left.	CTRL+ALT+LEFT ARROW
Move the insertion point right in the current page, or expand the page to the right.	CTRL+ALT+RIGHT ARROW
Go to the next note container.	ALT+DOWN ARROW
Go to the beginning of the line.	HOME
Go to the end of the line.	END
Move one character to the left.	LEFT ARROW
Move one character to the right.	RIGHT ARROW
Go back to the last page visited.	ALT+LEFT ARROW
Go forward to the next page visited.	ALT+RIGHT ARROW
Zoom in.	ALT+CTRL+PLUS SIGN (on the numeric keypad)

	−OR− ALT+CTRL+SHIFT+PLUS SIGN
Zoom out.	ALT+CTRL+MINUS SIGN (on the numeric keypad) −OR− ALT+CTRL+SHIFT+HYPHEN
Save changes. **Note:** While OneNote is running, your notes are automatically saved whenever you change them. Manually saving notes is not necessary.	CTRL+S

Working with notebooks and sections

TASK	SHORTCUT
Create a new section.	CTRL+T
Open a notebook.	CTRL+O
Open a section.	CTRL+ALT+SHIFT+O
Go to the next section.	CTRL+TAB
Go to the previous section.	CTRL+SHIFT+TAB
Go to the next page in the section.	CTRL+PAGE DOWN
Go to the previous page in the section.	CTRL+PAGE UP

Go to the first page in the section.	ALT+HOME
Go to the last page in the section.	ALT+END
Go to the first page in the currently visible set of page tabs.	ALT+PAGE UP
Go to the last page of the currently visible set of page tabs.	ALT+PAGE DOWN
Move or copy the current page.	CTRL+ALT+M
Put focus on the current page tab.	CTRL+ALT+G
Select the current page tab.	CTRL+SHFT+A
Put focus on the current section tab.	CTRL+SHIFT+G
Move the current section.	CTRL+SHIFT+G, SHIFT+F10, M
Switch to a different notebook on the Navigation bar.	CTRL+G, then press DOWN ARROW or UP ARROW keys to select a different notebook, and then press ENTER

Searching Notes

TASK	SHORTCUT
Move the insertion point to the **Search** box to search all notebooks.	CTRL+E

While searching all notebooks, preview the next result.	DOWN ARROW
While searching all notebooks, go to the selected result and dismiss Search.	ENTER
Change the search scope.	CTRL+E, TAB, SPACE
Open the Search Results pane.	ALT+O after searching
Search only the current page. **Note:** You can switch between searching everywhere and searching only the current page at any point by pressing CRTL+E or CTRL+F.	CTRL+F
While searching the current page, move to the next result.	ENTER or F3
While searching the current page, move to the previous result.	SHFT+F3
Dismiss Search and return to the page.	ESC

Sharing Notes

Sharing Notes With Other People

TASK	SHORTCUT
Send the selected pages in an e-mail message.	CTRL+SHIFT+E

Sharing Notes With Other Programs

TASK	SHORTCUT
Send the selected pages in an e-mail message.	CTRL+SHIFT+E
Create a **Today** Outlook task from the currently selected note.	CTRL+SHIFT+1

Create a **Tomorrow** Outlook task from the currently selected note.	CTRL+SHIFT+2
Create a **This Week** Outlook task from the currently selected note.	CTRL+SHIFT+3
Create a **Next Week** Outlook task from the currently selected note.	CTRL+SHIFT+4
Create a **No Date** Outlook task from the currently selected note.	CTRL+SHIFT+5
Open the selected Outlook task.	CTRL+SHIFT+K
Mark the selected Outlook task as complete.	CTRL+SHIFT+9
Delete the selected Outlook task.	CTRL+SHIFT+0
Sync changes in the current shared notebook.	SHIFT+F9
Sync changes in all shared notebooks.	F9
Mark the current page as Unread.	CTRL+Q

Protecting Notes.

Password-protecting sections

TASK	SHORTCUT
Lock all password-protected sections.	CTRL+ALT+L

Note: Some of the content in this topic may not be applicable to some languages.

CHAPTER 7

Keyboard Shortcuts For Use In Access 2010.

You can use keyboard shortcuts for quick access to frequently used commands or operations. The following sections list the keyboard shortcuts available in Microsoft Access 2010. You can also use keyboard shortcuts to move the focus to a menu, command, or control without using the mouse.

Definition of Program: Microsoft Access is a well-known electronic database program designed by Microsoft Corporation in 1997 which allows its users to create and manipulate database.

The following keyboard shortcuts will help you become a successful user of Microsoft OneNote 2010.

General Shortcut Keys

Opening Databases

TASK	SHORTCUT
Open a new database	CTRL+N
Open an existing database	CTRL+O

Printing And Saving

TASK	SHORTCUT
Print the current or selected object	CTRL+P

Open the **Print** dialog box from **Print Preview**	P or CTRL+P
Open the **Page Setup** dialog box from **Print Preview**	S
Cancel Print Preview or Layout Preview	C or ESC
Save a database object	CTRL+S or SHIFT+F12
Open the **Save As** dialog box	F12

Using a Combo Box or List Box

TASK	SHORTCUT
Open a combo box	F4 or ALT+DOWN ARROW
Refresh the contents of a Lookup field list box or combo box	F9
Move down one line	DOWN ARROW
Move down one page	PAGE DOWN
Move up one line	UP ARROW
Move up one page	PAGE UP
Exit the combo box or list box	TAB

Finding and Replacing Text or Data

TASK	SHORTCUT
Open the **Find** tab in the **Find and Replace** dialog box (Datasheet view and Form view only)	CTRL+F
Open the **Replace** tab in the **Find and Replace** dialog box (Datasheet view and Form view only)	CTRL+H
Find the next occurrence of the text specified in the **Find and Replace**	SHIFT+F4

dialog box when the dialog box is closed (Datasheet view and Form view only)	

Working in Design View

TASK	SHORTCUT
Switch between Edit mode (with insertion point displayed) and Navigation mode in a datasheet. When working in a form or report, press ESC to leave Navigation mode.	F2
Switch to the property sheet (Design view in forms and reports in both Access databases and Access projects)	F4
Switch to Form view from form Design view	F5
Switch between the upper and lower portions of a window (Design view of queries, and the Advanced Filter/Sort window)	F6
Cycle through the field grid, field properties, the Navigation Pane, access keys in the Keyboard Access System, Zoom controls, and the security bar (Design view of tables)	F6
Open the **Choose Builder** dialog box (Design view window of forms and reports)	F7
Open the Visual Basic Editor from a selected property in the property sheet for a form or report	F7
Switch from the Visual Basic Editor back to form or report Design view	SHIFT+F7 or ALT+F11

Editing Controls in Form and Report Design View

TASK	SHORTCUT
Copy the selected control to the Clipboard	CTRL+C
Cut the selected control and copy it to the Clipboard	CTRL+X
Paste the contents of the Clipboard in the upper-left corner of the selected section	CTRL+V
Move the selected control to the right (except controls that are part of a layout)	RIGHT ARROW or CTRL+RIGHT ARROW
Move the selected control to the left (except controls that are part of a layout)	LEFT ARROW or CTRL+LEFT ARROW
Move the selected control up	UP ARROW or CTRL+UP ARROW
Move the selected control down	DOWN ARROW or CTRL+DOWN ARROW
Increase the height of the selected control	SHIFT+DOWN ARROW
Increase the width of the selected control **Note:** If used with controls that are in a layout, the entire layout is resized	SHIFT+RIGHT ARROW
Reduce the height of the selected control	SHIFT+UP ARROW
Reduce the width of the selected control	SHIFT+LEFT ARROW

| **Note:** If used with controls that are in a layout, the entire layout is resized | |

Window Operations

By default, Microsoft Access 2010 databases display as tabbed documents. To use windowed documents, Click the **File** tab., and then click **Options**. In the **Access Options** dialog box, click **Current Database** and, under **Document Window Options**, click **Overlapping Windows**.

Note: You will have to close and reopen the current database for the option to take effect.

TASK	SHORTCUT
Toggle the Navigation Pane	F11
Cycle between open windows	CTRL+F6
Restore the selected minimized window when all windows are minimized	ENTER
Turn on Resize mode for the active window when it is not maximized; press the arrow keys to resize the window	CTRL+F8
Display the control menu	ALT+SPACEBAR
Display the shortcut menu	SHIFT+F10
Close the active window	CTRL+W or CTRL+F4
Switch between the Visual Basic Editor and the previous active window	ALT+F11

Working With Wizards

TASK	SHORTCUT
Toggle the focus forward between controls in the wizard	TAB
Move to the next page of the wizard	ALT+N
Move to the previous page of the wizard	ALT+B
Complete the wizard	ALT+F

Miscellaneous

TASK	SHORTCUT
Display the complete hyperlink address for a selected hyperlink	F2
Check spelling	F7
Open the Zoom box to conveniently enter expressions and other text in small input areas	SHIFT+F2
Display a property sheet in Design view	ALT+ENTER
Exit Access	ALT+F4
Invoke a Builder	CTRL+F2
Toggle forward between views when in a table, query, form, report, page, PivotTable list, PivotChart report, stored procedure, or Access project (.adp) function. If there are additional views available, successive keystrokes will move to the next available view.	CTRL+RIGHT ARROW or CRTL+COMMA (,)
Toggle back between views when in a table, query, form, report, page, PivotTable list, PivotChart report, stored procedure, or .adp function. If	CTRL+LEFT ARROW or CRTL+PERIOD (.)

there are additional views available, successive keystrokes will move to the previous view. **Note:** CTRL+PERIOD (.) does not work under all conditions with all objects.	

The Navigation Pane Shortcut Keys

TASK	SHORTCUT
Go to the Navigation Pane Search box from anywhere in the database.	ALT+CTRL+F

Editing and Navigating the Object List

TASK	SHORTCUT
Rename a selected object	F2
Move down one line	DOWN ARROW
Move down one window	PAGE DOWN
Move to the last object	END
Move up one line	UP ARROW
Move up one window	PAGE UP
Move to the first object	HOME

Navigating and Opening Objects

TASK	SHORTCUT
Open the selected table or query in Datasheet view	ENTER
Open the selected form or report	ENTER
Run the selected macro	ENTER
Open the selected table, query, form, report, data access page, macro, or module in Design view	CTRL+ENTER

Display the Immediate window in the Visual Basic Editor	CTRL+G

Work with Menus

TASK	SHORTCUT
Show the shortcut menu	SHIFT+F10
Show the access keys	ALT or F10
Show the program icon menu (on the program title bar)	ALT+SPACEBAR
With the menu or submenu visible, select the next or previous command	DOWN ARROW or UP ARROW
Select the menu to the left or right; or, when a submenu is visible, to switch between the main menu and the submenu	LEFT ARROW or RIGHT ARROW
Select the first or last command on the menu or submenu	HOME or END
Close the visible menu and submenu at the same time	ALT
Close the visible menu; or, with a submenu visible, to close the submenu only	ESC

Work in Windows and Dialog Boxes

Using a program window

TASK	SHORTCUT
Switch to the next program	ALT+TAB
Switch to the previous program	ALT+SHIFT+TAB
Show the Windows **Start** menu	CTRL+ESC
Close the active database window	CTRL+W
Switch to the next database window	CTRL+F6

Switch to the previous database window	CTRL+SHIFT+F6
Restore the selected minimized window when all windows are minimized	ENTER

Using a Dialog Box

TASK	SHORTCUT
Switch to the next tab in a dialog box	CTRL+TAB
Switch to the previous tab in a dialog box	CTRL+SHIFT+TAB
Move to the next option or option group	TAB
Move to the previous option or option group	SHIFT+TAB
Move between options in the selected drop-down list box, or to move between some options in a group of options	Arrow keys
Perform the action assigned to the selected button; select or clear the check box	SPACEBAR
Move to the option by the first letter in the option name in a drop-down list box	Letter key for the first letter in the option name you want (when a drop-down list box is selected)
Select the option, or to select or clear the check box by the letter	ALT+letter key

underlined in the option name	
Open the selected drop-down list box	ALT+DOWN ARROW
Close the selected drop-down list box	ESC
Perform the action assigned to the default button in the dialog box	ENTER
Cancel the command and close the dialog box	ESC

Editing in a Text Box

TASK	SHORTCUT
Move to the beginning of the entry	HOME
Move to the end of the entry	END
Move one character to the left or right	LEFT ARROW or RIGHT ARROW
Move one word to the left or right	CTRL+LEFT ARROW or CTRL+RIGHT ARROW
Select from the insertion point to the beginning of the text entry	SHIFT+HOME
Select from the insertion point to the end of the text entry	SHIFT+END
Change the selection by one character to the left	SHIFT+LEFT ARROW
Change the selection by one character to the right	SHIFT+RIGHT ARROW

Change the selection by one word to the left	CTRL+SHIFT+LEFT ARROW
Change the selection by one word to the right	CTRL+SHIFT+RIGHT ARROW

Work With Property Sheets

Using a property sheet with a form or report in Design view

TASK	SHORTCUT
Toggle the property sheet tab	F4
Move among choices in the control drop-down list one item at a time	DOWN ARROW or UP ARROW
Move among choices in the control drop-down list five items at a time	PAGE DOWN or PAGE UP
Move to the property sheet tabs from the control drop-down list	TAB
Move among the property sheet tabs with a tab selected, but no property selected	LEFT ARROW or RIGHT ARROW
With a property already selected, move down one property on a tab	TAB
With a property selected, move up one property on a tab; or if already at the top, move to the tab	SHIFT+TAB
Toggle forward between tabs when a property is selected	CTRL+TAB
Toggle backward between tabs when a property is selected	CTRL+SHIFT+TAB

Using a property sheet with a table or query

TASK	SHORTCUT
Toggle the property sheet tab	F4
With a tab selected, but no property selected, move among the property sheet tabs	LEFT ARROW or RIGHT ARROW
Move to the property sheet tabs when a property is selected	CTRL+TAB
Move to the first property of a tab when no property is selected	TAB
Move down one property on a tab	TAB
Move up one property on a tab; or if already at the top, select the tab itself	SHIFT+TAB
Toggle forward between tabs when a property is selected	CTRL+TAB
Toggle backward between tabs when a property is selected	CTRL+SHIFT+TAB

Work With the Field List Pane

TASK	SHORTCUT
Toggle the **Field List** pane	ALT+F8
Add the selected field to the form or report detail section	ENTER
Move up or down the **Field List** pane	UP ARROW or DOWN ARROW
Move to the upper **Field List** pane from the lower pane	SHIFT+TAB

Move to the lower **Field List** pane from the upper pane	TAB

Keyboard Shortcuts for Using the Help Window

TASK	SHORTCUT
Select the next hidden text or hyperlink, or **Show All** or **Hide All** at the top of a topic	TAB
Select the previous hidden text or hyperlink, or the **Browser View** button at the top of a Microsoft Office Web site article	SHIFT+TAB
Perform the action for the selected **Show All**, **Hide All**, hidden text, or hyperlink	ENTER
Move back to the previous Help topic	ALT+LEFT ARROW
Move forward to the next Help topic	ALT+RIGHT ARROW
Open the **Print** dialog box	CTRL+P
Scroll small amounts up and down, respectively, within the currently-displayed Help topic.	UP ARROW AND DOWN ARROW
Scroll larger amounts up and down, respectively, within the currently-displayed Help topic.	PAGE UP AND PAGE DOWN
Display a menu of commands for the Help window; requires that the Help window have active focus (click an item in the Help window).	SHIFT+F10

Keys For Working With Text And Data

Select Text and Data

Selecting Text in a field

TASK	SHORTCUT
Change the size of the selection by one character to the right	SHIFT+RIGHT ARROW
Change the size of the selection by one word to the right	CTRL+SHIFT+RIGHT ARROW
Change the size of the selection by one character to the left	SHIFT+LEFT ARROW
Change the size of the selection by one word to the left	CTRL+SHIFT+LEFT ARROW

Selecting a Field or Record

Note: To cancel a selection, use the opposite arrow key.

TASK	SHORTCUT
Select the next field	TAB
Switch between Edit mode (with insertion point displayed) and Navigation mode in a datasheet. When using a form or report, press ESC to leave Navigation mode.	F2

Switch between selecting the current record and the first field of the current record, in Navigation mode	SHIFT+SPACEBAR
Extend selection to the previous record, if the current record is selected	SHIFT+UP ARROW
Extend selection to the next record, if the current record is selected	SHIFT+DOWN ARROW
Select all records	CTRL+A or CTRL+SHIFT+SPACEBAR

Extending a Selection

TASK	SHORTCUT
Turn on Extend mode (in Datasheet view, **Extended Selection** appears in the lower-right corner of the window); pressing F8 repeatedly extends the selection to the word, the field, the record, and all records	F8
Extend a selection to adjacent fields in the same row in Datasheet view	LEFT ARROW or RIGHT ARROW
Extend a selection to adjacent rows in Datasheet view	UP ARROW or DOWN ARROW
Undo the previous extension	SHIFT+F8
Cancel Extend mode	ESC

Selecting and Moving a Column in Datasheet View.

TASK	SHORTCUT
Select the current column or cancel the column selection, in Navigation mode only	CTRL+SPACEBAR
Select the column to the right, if the current column is selected	SHIFT+RIGHT ARROW
Select the column to the left, if the current column is selected	SHIFT+LEFT ARROW
Turn on Move mode; then press the RIGHT ARROW or LEFT ARROW key to move selected column(s) to the right or left	CTRL+SHIFT+F8

Edit Text and Data

Note: If the insertion point is not visible, press F2 to display it.

Moving the Insertion Point in a Field

TASK	SHORTCUT
Move the insertion point one character to the right	RIGHT ARROW
Move the insertion point one word to the right	CTRL+RIGHT ARROW
Move the insertion point one character to the left	LEFT ARROW
Move the insertion point one word to the left	CTRL+LEFT ARROW
Move the insertion point to the end of the field, in single-line fields; or to move it to the end of the line in multi-line fields	END
Move the insertion point to the end of the field, in multiple-line fields	CTRL+END

Move the insertion point to the beginning of the field, in single-line fields; or to move it to the beginning of the line in multi-line fields	HOME
Move the insertion point to the beginning of the field, in multiple-line fields	CTRL+HOME

Copying, Moving, or Deleting Text

TASK	SHORTCUT
Copy the selection to the Clipboard	CTRL+C
Cut the selection and copy it to the Clipboard	CTRL+X
Paste the contents of the Clipboard at the insertion point	CTRL+V
Delete the selection or the character to the left of the insertion point	BACKSPACE
Delete the selection or the character to the right of the insertion point	DELETE
Delete all characters to the right of the insertion point	CTRL+DELETE

Undoing Changes

TASK	SHORTCUT
Undo typing	CTRL+Z or ALT+BACKSPACE
Undo changes in the current field or current record; if both have been changed, press ESC twice to undo changes, first in the current field and then in the current record	ESC

Entering Data in Datasheet or Form View

TASK	SHORTCUT
Insert the current date	CTRL+SEMICOLON (;)
Insert the current time	CTRL+SHIFT+COLON (:)
Insert the default value for a field	CTRL+ALT+SPACEBAR
Insert the value from the same field in the previous record	CTRL+APOSTROPHE (')
Add a new record	CTRL+PLUS SIGN (+)
In a datasheet, delete the current record	CTRL+MINUS SIGN (-)
Save changes to the current record	SHIFT+ENTER
Switch between the values in a check box or option button	SPACEBAR
Insert a new line	CTRL+ENTER

Refreshing Fields with Current Data

TASK	SHORTCUT
Recalculate the fields in the window	F9
Requery the underlying tables; in a subform, this requeries the underlying table for the subform only	SHIFT+F9
Refresh the contents of a Lookup field list box or combo box	F9

Keys For Navigating Records.

Navigate in Design View

TASK	SHORTCUT
Switch between Edit mode (with insertion point displayed) and Navigation mode	F2
Toggle the property sheet	F4
Switch to Form view from form Design view	F5
Switch between the upper and lower portions of a window (Design view of macros, queries, and the Advanced Filter/Sort window) Use F6 when the TAB key does not take you to the section of the screen you want.	F6
Toggle forward between the design pane, properties, Navigation Pane, access keys, and Zoom controls (Design view of tables, forms, and reports)	F6
Open the Visual Basic Editor from a selected property in the property sheet for a form or report	F7
Invokes the **Field List** pane in a form, report, or data access page. If the **Field List** pane is already open, focus moves to the **Field List** pane.	ALT+F8
When you have a code module open, switch from the Visual Basic Editor to form or report Design view	SHIFT+F7
Switch from a control's property sheet in form or report Design view to the	SHIFT+F7

design surface without changing the control focus	
Display a property sheet	ALT+ENTER
Copy the selected control to the Clipboard	CTRL+C
Cut the selected control and copy it to the Clipboard	CTRL+X
Paste the contents of the Clipboard in the upper-left corner of the selected section	CTRL+V
Move the selected control to the right by a pixel along the page's grid	RIGHT ARROW
Move the selected control to the left by a pixel along the page's grid	LEFT ARROW
Move the selected control up by a pixel along the page's grid **Note:** For controls in a stacked layout, this switches the position of the selected control with the control directly above it, unless it is already the uppermost control in the layout.	UP ARROW
Move the selected control down by a pixel along the page's grid **Note:** For controls in a stacked layout, this switches the position of the selected control with the control directly below it, unless it is already the lowermost control in the layout.	DOWN ARROW
Move the selected control to the right by a pixel (irrespective of the page's grid)	CTRL+RIGHT ARROW

Move the selected control to the left by a pixel (irrespective of the page's grid)	CTRL+LEFT ARROW
Move the selected control up by a pixel (irrespective of the page's grid) **Note:** For controls in a stacked layout, this switches the position of the selected control with the control directly above it, unless it is already the uppermost control in the layout.	CTRL+UP ARROW
Move the selected control down by a pixel (irrespective of the page's grid) **Note:** For controls in a stacked layout, this switches the position of the selected control with the control directly below it, unless it is already the lowermost control in the layout.	CTRL+DOWN ARROW
Increase the width of the selected control (to the right) by a pixel **Note:** For controls in a stacked layout, this increases the width of the whole layout.	SHIFT+RIGHT ARROW
Decrease the width of the selected control (to the left) by a pixel **Note:** For controls in a stacked layout, this decreases the width of the whole layout.	SHIFT+LEFT ARROW
Decrease the height of the selected control (from the bottom) by a pixel	SHIFT+UP ARROW
Increase the height of the selected control (from the bottom) by a pixel	SHIFT+DOWN ARROW

Navigate in Datasheet view

Going to a Specific Record

TASK	SHORTCUT
Move to the record number box; then type the record number and press ENTER	F5

Navigating Between Fields and Records

TASK	SHORTCUT
Move to the next field	TAB or RIGHT ARROW
Move to the last field in the current record, in Navigation mode	END
Move to the previous field	SHIFT+TAB, or LEFT ARROW
Move to the first field in the current record, in Navigation mode	HOME
Move to the current field in the next record	DOWN ARROW
Move to the current field in the last record, in Navigation mode	CTRL+DOWN ARROW
Move to the last field in the last record, in Navigation mode	CTRL+END
Move to the current field in the previous record	UP ARROW
Move to the current field in the first record, in Navigation mode	CTRL+UP ARROW
Move to the first field in the first record, in Navigation mode	CTRL+HOME

Navigating to Another Screen of Data

TASK	SHORTCUT
Move down one screen	PAGE DOWN
Move up one screen	PAGE UP
Move right one screen	CTRL+PAGE DOWN
Move left one screen	CTRL+PAGE UP

Navigate in Subdatasheets

Going to a specific record

TASK	SHORTCUT
Move from the subdatasheet to move to the record number box; then type the record number and press ENTER	ALT+F5

Expanding and Collapsing Subdatasheet

TASK	SHORTCUT
Move from the datasheet to expand the record's Subdatasheet	CTRL+SHIFT+DOWN ARROW
Collapse the subdatasheet	CTRL+SHIFT+UP ARROW

Navigating between the datasheet and subdatasheet

TASK	SHORTCUT
Enter the subdatasheet from the last field of the previous record in the datasheet	TAB

Enter the subdatasheet from the first field of the following record in the datasheet	SHIFT+TAB
Exit the subdatasheet and move to the first field of the next record in the datasheet	CTRL+TAB
Exit the subdatasheet and move to the last field of the previous record in the datasheet	CTRL+SHIFT+TAB
From the last field in the subdatasheet to enter the next field in the datasheet	TAB
From the datasheet to bypass the subdatasheet and move to the next record in the datasheet	DOWN ARROW
From the datasheet to bypass the subdatasheet and move to the previous record in the datasheet	UP ARROW

Note: You can navigate between fields and records in a subdatasheet with the same shortcut keys used in Datasheet view.

Navigate in Form View

Going to a specific record

TASK	SHORTCUT
Move to the record number box; then type the record number and press ENTER	F5

Navigating Between Fields and Records

TASK	SHORTCUT
Move to the next field	TAB
Move to the previous field	SHIFT+TAB
Move to the last control on the form and remain in the current record, in Navigation mode	END
Move to the last control on the form and set focus in the last record, in Navigation mode	CTRL+END
Move to the first control on the form and remain in the current record, in Navigation mode	HOME
Move to the first control on the form and set focus in the first record, in Navigation mode	CTRL+HOME
Move to the current field in the next record	CTRL+PAGE DOWN
Move to the current field in the previous record	CTRL+PAGE UP

Navigating In Forms With More Than One Page

TASK	SHORTCUT
Move down one page; at the end of the record, moves to the equivalent page on the next record	PAGE DOWN
Move up one page; at the end of the record, moves to the equivalent page on the previous record	PAGE UP

Navigating Between The Main Form And Subform

TASK	SHORTCUT
Enter the subform from the preceding field in the main form	TAB
Enter the subform from the following field in the main form	SHIFT+TAB
Exit the subform and move to the next field in the master form or next record	CTRL+TAB
Exit the subform and move to the previous field in the main form or previous record	CTRL+SHIFT+TAB

Navigate in Print Preview and Layout Preview

Dialog box and window operations

TASK	SHORTCUT
Open the **Print** dialog box from Print	CTRL+P (or datasheets, forms, and reports)
Open the **Page Setup** dialog box (forms and reports only)	S
Zoom in or out on a part of the page	Z
Cancel Print Preview or Layout Preview	C or ESC

Viewing different pages

TASK	SHORTCUT
Move to the page number box; then type the page number and press ENTER	ALT+F5

View the next page (when **Fit To Window** is selected)	PAGE DOWN or DOWN ARROW
View the previous page (when **Fit To Window** is selected)	PAGE UP or UP ARROW

Navigating in Print Preview and Layout Preview

TASK	SHORTCUT
Scroll down in small increments	DOWN ARROW
Scroll down one full screen	PAGE DOWN
Move to the bottom of the page	CTRL+DOWN ARROW
Scroll up in small increments	UP ARROW
Scroll up one full screen	PAGE UP
Move to the top of the page	CTRL+UP ARROW
Scroll to the right in small increments	RIGHT ARROW
Move to the right edge of the page	END
Move to the lower-right corner of the page	CTRL+END
Scroll to the left in small increments	LEFT ARROW
Move to the left edge of the page	HOME
Move to the upper-left corner of the page	CTRL+HOME

Navigate in the Database Diagram window in an Access project

TASK	SHORTCUT
Move from a table cell to the table's title bar	ESC
Move from a table's title bar to the last cell you edited	ENTER

Move from table title bar to table title bar, or from cell to cell inside a table	TAB
Expand a list inside a table	ALT + DOWN ARROW
Scroll through the items in a drop-down list from top to bottom	DOWN ARROW
Move to the previous item in a list	UP ARROW
Select an item in a list and move to the next cell	ENTER
Change the setting in a check box	SPACEBAR
Go to the first cell in the row, or to the beginning of the current cell	HOME
Go to the last cell in the row, or to the end of the current cell	END
Scroll to the next "page" inside a table, or to the next "page" of the diagram	PAGE DOWN
Scroll to the previous "page" inside a table, or to the previous "page" of the diagram	PAGE UP

Navigate in the Query Designer in an Access project

Any Pane

TASK	SHORTCUT
Move among the Query Designer panes	F6, SHIFT+F6

Diagram Pane

TASK	SHORTCUT
Move among tables, views, and functions, (and to join lines, if available)	TAB, or SHIFT+TAB
Move between columns in a table, view, or function	Arrow keys
Choose the selected data column for output	SPACEBAR or PLUS key
Remove the selected data column from the query output	SPACEBAR or MINUS key
Remove the selected table, view, or function, or join line from the query	DELETE

Note: If multiple items are selected, pressing SPACEBAR affects all selected items. Select multiple items by holding down the SHIFT key while clicking them. Toggle the selected state of a single item by holding down CTRL while clicking it.

Grid Pane

TASK	SHORTCUT
Move among cells	Arrow keys or TAB or SHIFT+TAB
Move to the last row in the current column	CTRL+DOWN ARROW
Move to the first row in the current column	CTRL+UP ARROW
Move to the top left cell in the visible portion of grid	CTRL+HOME
Move to the bottom right cell	CTRL+END
Move in a drop-down list	UP ARROW or DOWN ARROW

Select an entire grid column	CTRL+SPACEBAR
Toggle between edit mode and cell selection mode	F2
Copy selected text in cell to the Clipboard (in edit mode)	CTRL+C
Cut selected text in cell and place it on the Clipboard (in edit mode)	CTRL+X
Paste text from the Clipboard (in edit mode)	CTRL+V
Toggle between insert and overstrike mode while editing in a cell	INS
Toggle the check box in the Output column**Note** If multiple items are selected, pressing this key affects all selected items.	SPACEBAR
Clear the selected contents of a cell	DELETE
Remove row containing selected data column from the query **Note** If multiple items are selected, pressing this key affects all selected items.	DELETE
Clear all values for a selected grid column	DELETE
Insert row between existing rows	INS (after you select grid row)
Add an Or ... column	INS (after you select any Or ... column)

SQL Pane

You can use the standard Windows editing keys when working in the SQL pane, such as CTRL+ arrow keys to move between words, and the **Cut**, **Copy**, and **Paste** commands on the **Edit** menu.

Note: You can only insert text; there is no overstrike mode.

Work with PivotTable Views

PivotTable view

Keys for selecting elements in PivotTable view

TASK	SHORTCUT
Move the selection from left to right, and then down	The TAB key
Move the selection from top to bottom, and then to the right	ENTER
Select the cell to the left. If the current cell is the leftmost cell, SHIFT+TAB selects the last cell in the previous row.	SHIFT+TAB
Select the cell above the current cell. If the current cell is the topmost cell, SHIFT+ENTER selects the last cell in the previous column.	SHIFT+ENTER
Select the detail cells for the next item in the row area	CTRL+ENTER

Select the detail cells for the previous item in the row area	SHIFT+CTRL+ENTER
Move the selection in the direction of the arrow key. If a row or column field is selected, press DOWN ARROW to move to the first item of data in the field, and then press an arrow key to move to the next or previous item or back to the field. If a detail field is selected, press DOWN ARROW or RIGHT ARROW to move to the first cell in the detail area.	Arrow keys
Extend or reduce the selection in the direction of the arrow key	SHIFT+arrow keys
Move the selection to the last cell in the direction of the arrow key	CTRL+arrow keys
Move the selected item in the direction of the arrow key	SHIFT+ALT+arrow keys
Select the leftmost cell of the current row	HOME
Select the rightmost cell of the current row	END
Select the leftmost cell of the first row	CTRL+HOME
Select the last cell of the last row	CTRL+END
Extend selection to the leftmost cell of the first row	SHIFT+CTRL+HOME
Extend selection to the last cell of the last row	SHIFT+CTRL+END

Select the field for the currently selected item of data, total, or detail	CTRL+SPACEBAR
Select the entire row containing the currently selected cell	SHIFT+SPACEBAR
Select the entire PivotTable view	CTRL+A
Display the next screen	PAGE DOWN
Display the previous screen	PAGE UP
Extend the selection down one screen	SHIFT+PAGE DOWN
Reduce the selection by one screen	SHIFT+PAGE UP
Display the next screen to the right	ALT+PAGE DOWN
Display the previous screen to the left	ALT+PAGE UP
Extend the selection to the page on the right	SHIFT+ALT+PAGE DOWN
Extend the selection to the page on the left	SHIFT+ALT+PAGE UP

Keys For Carrying Out Commands

TASK	SHORTCUT
Display Help topics	F1
Display the shortcut menu for the selected element of the PivotTable view. Use the shortcut menus to carry out commands in the PivotTable view.	SHIFT+F10
Carry out a command on the shortcut menu	Underlined letter

Close the shortcut menu without carrying out a command	ESC
Display the **Properties** dialog box	ALT+ENTER
Cancel a refresh operation in progress	ESC
Copy the selected data from the PivotTable view to the Clipboard	CTRL+C
Export the contents of the PivotTable view to Microsoft Excel 2010Excel 2010	CTRL+E

Keys for displaying, hiding, filtering, or sorting data

TASK	SHORTCUT
Show or hide the expand indicators (⊟ boxes) beside items	CTRL+8
Expand the currently selected item	CTRL+PLUS SIGN (on the numeric keypad)
Hide the currently selected item	CTRL+MINUS SIGN (on the numeric keypad)
Open the list for the currently selected field	ALT+DOWN ARROW
Alternately move to the most recently selected item, the **OK** button, and the **Cancel** button in the drop-down list for a field	The TAB key
Move to the next item in the drop-down list for a field	Arrow keys
Select or clear the check box for the current item in the drop-down list for a field	SPACEBAR

Close the drop-down list for a field and apply any changes you made	ENTER
Close the drop-down list for a field without applying your changes	ESC
Turn AutoFilter on or off	CTRL+T
Sort data in the selected field or total in ascending order (A – Z o – 9)	CTRL+SHIFT+A
Sort data in the selected field or total in descending order (Z – A 9 – o)	CTRL+SHIFT+Z
Move the selected member up or left	ALT+SHIFT+UP ARROW or ALT+SHIFT+LEFT ARROW
Move the selected member down or right	ALT+SHIFT+DOWN ARROW or ALT+SHIFT+RIGHT ARROW

Keys for working with the Field List pane

TASK	SHORTCUT
Display the **Field List** pane, or activate it if it is already displayed	CTRL+L
Move to the next item in the **Field List** pane	Arrow keys
Move to the previous item and include it in the selection	SHIFT+UP ARROW
Move to the next item and include it in the selection	SHIFT+DOWN ARROW

Move to the previous item, but don't include the item in the selection	CTRL+UP ARROW
Move to the next item, but don't include the item in the selection	CTRL+DOWN ARROW
Remove the item from the selection, if the item that has focus is included in the selection, and vice versa	CTRL+SPACEBAR
Expand the current item in the **Field List** pane to display its contents. Or expand Totals to display the available total fields.	PLUS SIGN (numeric keypad)
Collapse the current item in the **Field List** pane to hide its contents. Or collapse Totals to hide the available total fields.	MINUS SIGN (numeric keypad)
Alternately move to the most recently selected item, the **Add to** button, and the list next to the **Add to** button in the **Field List** pane	The TAB key
Open the drop-down list next to the **Add to** button in the **Field List** pane. Use the arrow keys to move to the next item in the list, and then press ENTER to select an item.	ALT+DOWN ARROW
Add the highlighted field in the **Field List** pane to the area in the PivotTable view that is displayed in the **Add to** list	ENTER

Keys for adding fields and totals

TASK	SHORTCUT
Add a new total field for the selected field in the PivotTable view by using the **Sum** summary function	CTRL+SHIFT+S
Add a new total field for the selected field in the PivotTable view by using the **Count** summary function	CTRL+SHIFT+C
Add a new total field for the selected field in the PivotTable view by using the **Min** summary function	CTRL+SHIFT+M
Add a new total field for the selected field in the PivotTable view by using the **Max** summary function	CTRL+SHIFT+X
Add a new total field for the selected field in the PivotTable view by using the **Average** summary function	CTRL+SHIFT+E
Add a new total field for the selected field in the PivotTable view by using the **Standard Deviation** summary function	CTRL+SHIFT+D
Add a new total field for the selected field in the PivotTable view by using the **Standard Deviation Population** summary function	CTRL+SHIFT+T
Add a new total field for the selected field in the PivotTable view by using the **Variance** summary function	CTRL+SHIFT+V
Add a new total field for the selected field in the PivotTable view by using the **Variance Population** summary function	CTRL+SHIFT+R

Turn subtotals and grand totals on or off for the selected field in the PivotTable view	CTRL+SHIFT+B
Add a calculated detail field	CTRL+F

Keys for changing the layout

Note: The following four shortcuts do not work if you press the keys 1, 2, 3, or 4 from the numeric pad of your keyboard.

TASK	SHORTCUT
Move the selected field in the PivotTable view to the row area	CTRL+1
Move the selected field in the PivotTable view to the column area	CTRL+2
Move the selected field in the PivotTable view to the filter area	CTRL+3
Move the selected field in the PivotTable view to the detail area	CTRL+4
Move the selected row or column field in the PivotTable view to a higher level	CTRL+LEFT ARROW
Move the selected row or column field in the PivotTable view to a lower level	CTRL+RIGHT ARROW

Keys for formatting elements in PivotTable view

To use the following shortcuts, first select a detail field or a data cell for a total field.

The first seven keyboard shortcuts change the number format of the selected field.

TASK	SHORTCUT
Apply the general number format to values in the selected total or detail field	CTRL+SHIFT+~ (tilde)
Apply the currency format, with two decimal places and negative numbers in parentheses, to values in the selected total or detail field	CTRL+SHIFT+$
Apply the percentage format, with no decimal places, to values in the selected total or detail field	CTRL+SHIFT+%
Apply the exponential number format, with two decimal places, to values in the selected total or detail field	CTRL+SHIFT+^
Apply the date format, with the day, month, and year, to values in the selected total or detail field	CTRL+SHIFT+#
Apply the time format, with the hour, minute, and AM or PM, to values in the selected total or detail field	CTRL+SHIFT+@
Apply the numeric format, with two decimal places, thousands separator, and a minus sign for negative values, to values in the selected total or detail field	CTRL+SHIFT+!
Make text bold in the selected field of the PivotTable view	CTRL+B
Make text underlined in the selected field of the PivotTable view	CTRL+U
Make text italic in the selected field of the PivotTable view	CTRL+I

PivotChart view

Keys for selecting items in a chart

TASK	SHORTCUT
Select the next item in the chart	RIGHT ARROW
Select the previous item in the chart	LEFT ARROW
Select the next group of items	DOWN ARROW
Select the previous group of items	UP ARROW

Keys for working with properties and options

TASK	SHORTCUT
Display the **Properties** dialog box	ALT+ENTER
When the **Properties** dialog box is active, select the next item on the active tab	**The TAB key**
When a tab in the **Properties** dialog box is active, select the next tab	RIGHT ARROW
When a tab in the **Properties** dialog box is active, select the previous tab	LEFT ARROW
Display a list or palette when a button that contains a list or palette is selected	DOWN ARROW
Display the shortcut menu	SHIFT+F10
Carry out a command on the shortcut menu	Underlined letter
Close the shortcut menu without carrying out a command	ESC

Keys for working with fields

TASK	SHORTCUT
Open the list for the currently selected field	ALT+DOWN ARROW
In the drop-down list for a field, alternately move to the most recently selected item, the **OK** button, and the **Cancel** button	The TAB key
In the drop-down list for a field, move to the next item	Arrow keys
In the drop-down list for a field, select or clear the check box for the current item	SPACEBAR
Close the drop-down list for a field and apply any changes you made	ENTER
Close the drop-down list for a field without applying your changes	ESC

Keys for working with the Field List pane

TASK	SHORTCUT
Display the **Field List** pane, or activate it if it is already displayed	CTRL+L
Move to the next item in the **Field List** pane	Arrow keys
Move to the previous item and include it in the selection	SHIFT+UP ARROW
Move to the next item and include it in the selection	SHIFT+DOWN ARROW
Move to the previous item, but don't include the item in the selection	CTRL+UP ARROW
Move to the next item, but don't include the item in the selection	CTRL+DOWN ARROW

Remove the item from the selection if the item that has focus is included in the selection, and vice versa	CTRL+SPACEBAR
Expand the current item in the **Field List** pane to display its contents, or expand Totals to display the available total fields	PLUS SIGN (numeric keypad)
Collapse the current item in the **Field List** pane to hide its contents, or collapse Totals to hide the available total fields.	MINUS SIGN (numeric keypad)
In the **Field List** pane, alternately move to the most recently selected item, the **Add to** button, and the list next to the **Add to** button	The TAB key
Open the drop-down list next to the **Add to** button in the **Field List** pane. Use the arrow keys to move to the next item in the list, and then press ENTER to select an item.	ALT+DOWN ARROW
Add the highlighted field in the **Field List** pane to the drop area that is displayed in the **Add to** list	ENTER

Microsoft Office Fluent Ribbon.

Office Fluent Ribbon

1. Press ALT.

   The KeyTips are displayed over each feature that is available in the current view.

2. Press the letter shown in the KeyTip over the feature that you want to use.
3. Depending on which letter you press, you might be shown additional KeyTips. For example, if the **External Data** tab is active and you press C, the **Create** tab is displayed, along with the KeyTips for the groups on that tab.
4. Continue pressing letters until you press the letter of the command or control that you want to use. In some cases, you must first press the letter of the group that contains the command.

Note: To cancel the action that you are taking and hide the KeyTips, press ALT.

Online Help.

Keyboard shortcuts for using the Help window

The Help window provides access to all Office Help content. The Help window displays topics and other Help content.

In the Help Window

TASK	SHORTCUT
Open the Help window.	F1
Switch between the Help window and the active program.	ALT+TAB
Go back to **Program Name** Home.	ALT+HOME
Select the next item in the Help window.	TAB
Select the previous item in the Help window.	SHIFT+TAB

Perform the action for the selected item.	ENTER
In the **Browse Program Name Help** section of the Help window, select the next or previous item, respectively.	TAB or SHIFT+TAB
In the **Browse Program Name Help** section of the Help window, expand or collapse the selected item, respectively.	ENTER
Select the next hidden text or hyperlink, including **Show All** or **Hide All** at the top of a topic.	TAB
Select the previous hidden text or hyperlink.	SHIFT+TAB
Perform the action for the selected **Show All**, **Hide All**, hidden text, or hyperlink.	ENTER
Move back to the previous Help topic (**Back** button).	ALT+LEFT ARROW or BACKSPACE
Move forward to the next Help topic (**Forward** button).	ALT+RIGHT ARROW
Scroll small amounts up or down, respectively, within the currently displayed Help topic.	UP ARROW, DOWN ARROW
Scroll larger amounts up or down, respectively, within the currently displayed Help topic.	PAGE UP, PAGE DOWN
Display a menu of commands for the Help window. This requires that the Help window have the active focus (click in the Help window).	SHIFT+F10

Stop the last action (**Stop** button).	ESC
Refresh the window (**Refresh** button).	F5
Print the current Help topic. **Note:** If the cursor is not in the current Help topic, press F6, and then press CTRL+P.	CTRL+P
Change the connection state.	F6, and then press ENTER to open the list of choices
Switch among areas in the Help window; for example, switch between the toolbar and the **Search** list.	F6
In a Table of Contents in tree view, select the next or previous item, respectively.	UP ARROW, DOWN ARROW
In a Table of Contents in tree view, expand or collapse the selected item, respectively.	LEFT ARROW, RIGHT ARROW

Microsoft Office Basics.

Display and use windows

TASK	SHORTCUT
Switch to the next window.	ALT+TAB
Switch to the previous window.	ALT+SHIFT+TAB
Close the active window.	CTRL+W or CTRL+F4

Move to a task pane from another pane in the program window (clockwise direction). You might need to press F6 more than once. **Note:** If pressing F6 doesn't display the task pane you want, try pressing ALT to place focus on the menu bar or Microsoft Office Fluent Ribbon and then pressing CTRL+TAB to move to the task pane.	F6
When more than one window is open, switch to the next window.	CTRL+F6
Switch to the previous window.	CTRL+SHIFT+F6
When a document window is not maximized, perform the **Size** command (on the **Control** menu for the window). Press the arrow keys to resize the window, and, when finished, press ENTER.	CTRL+F8
Minimize a window to an icon (works for only some Microsoft Office programs).	CTRL+F9
Maximize or restore a selected window.	CTRL+F10
Copy a picture of the screen to the Clipboard.	PRINT SCREEN
Copy a picture of the selected window to the Clipboard.	ALT+PRINT SCREEN

Move around in text or cells

TASK	SHORTCUT
Move one character to the left.	LEFT ARROW

Move one character to the right.	RIGHT ARROW
Move one line up.	UP ARROW
Move one line down.	DOWN ARROW
Move one word to the left.	CTRL+LEFT ARROW
Move one word to the right.	CTRL+RIGHT ARROW
Move to the end of a line.	END
Move to the beginning of a line.	HOME
Move up one paragraph.	CTRL+UP ARROW
Move down one paragraph.	CTRL+DOWN ARROW
Move to the end of a text box.	CTRL+END
Move to the beginning of a text box.	CTRL+HOME
Repeat the last **Find** action.	SHIFT+F4

Move around in and work in tables

TASK	SHORTCUT
Move to the next cell.	TAB
Move to the preceding cell.	SHIFT+TAB
Move to the next row.	DOWN ARROW
Move to the preceding row.	UP ARROW
Insert a tab in a cell.	CTRL+TAB
Start a new paragraph.	ENTER
Add a new row at the bottom of the table.	TAB at the end of the last row

Access and use task panes

TASK	SHORTCUT
Move to a task pane from another pane in the program window. (You	F6

might need to press F6 more than once.) **Note:** If pressing F6 doesn't display the task pane you want, try pressing ALT to place focus on the menu bar and then pressing CTRL+TAB to move to the task pane.	
When a menu or toolbar is active, move to a task pane. (You might need to press CTRL+TAB more than once.)	CTRL+TAB
When a task pane is active, select the next or previous option in the task pane.	TAB or SHIFT+TAB
Display the full set of commands on the task pane menu.	CTRL+DOWN ARROW
Move among choices on a selected submenu; move among certain options in a group of options in a dialog box.	DOWN ARROW or UP ARROW
Open the selected menu, or perform the action assigned to the selected button.	SPACEBAR or ENTER
Open a shortcut menu; open a drop-down menu for the selected gallery item.	SHIFT+F10
When a menu or submenu is visible, select the first or last command on the menu or submenu.	HOME or END
Scroll up or down in the selected gallery list.	PAGE UP or PAGE DOWN
Move to the top or bottom of the selected gallery list.	CTRL+HOME or CTRL+END

Tips

Resize and move toolbars, menus, and task panes

1. Press ALT to select the menu bar.
2. Press CTRL+TAB repeatedly to select the toolbar or task pane that you want.
3. Do one of the following:

Resize a toolbar

    a. On the toolbar, press CTRL+SPACEBAR to display the **Toolbar Options** menu.

    b. Click the **Size** command, and then press ENTER.

    c. Use the arrow keys to resize the toolbar. Press CTRL+ the arrow keys to resize one pixel at a time.

Move a toolbar

    d. On the toolbar, press CTRL+SPACEBAR to display the **Toolbar Options** menu.

    e. Click the **Move** command, and then press ENTER.

    f. Use the arrow keys to position the toolbar. Press CTRL+ the arrow keys to move one pixel at a time. To undock the toolbar, press the DOWN ARROW repeatedly. To dock the toolbar vertically on the left or right side, press the LEFT ARROW or the RIGHT ARROW, respectively, when the toolbar is positioned all the way to the left or the right side.

Resize a task pane

g. In the task pane, press CTRL+SPACEBAR to display a menu of additional commands.
h. Use the DOWN ARROW key to select the **Size** command, and then press ENTER.
i. Use the arrow keys to resize the task pane. Use CTRL+ the arrow keys to resize one pixel at a time.

Move a task pane

j. In the task pane, press CTRL+SPACEBAR to display a menu of additional commands.
k. Use the DOWN ARROW key to select the **Move** command, and then press ENTER.
l. Use the arrow keys to position the task pane. Use CTRL+ the arrow keys to move one pixel at a time.
4. When you finish moving or resizing, press ESC.

Use dialog boxes

TASK	SHORTCUT
Move to the next option or option group.	TAB
Move to the previous option or option group.	SHIFT+TAB
Switch to the next tab in a dialog box.	CTRL+TAB
Switch to the previous tab in a dialog box.	CTRL+SHIFT+TAB
Move between options in an open drop-down list, or	Arrow keys

between options in a group of options.	
Perform the action assigned to the selected button; select or clear the selected check box.	SPACEBAR
Open the list if it is closed and move to that option in the list.	First letter of an option in a drop-down list
Select an option; select or clear a check box.	ALT+ the letter underlined in an option
Open a selected drop-down list.	ALT+DOWN ARROW
Close a selected drop-down list; cancel a command and close a dialog box.	ESC
Perform the action assigned to a default button in a dialog box.	ENTER

Use edit boxes within dialog boxes

An edit box is a blank in which you type or paste an entry, such as your user name or the path of a folder.

TASK	SHORTCUT
Move to the beginning of the entry.	HOME
Move to the end of the entry.	END
Move one character to the left or right.	LEFT ARROW or RIGHT ARROW
Move one word to the left.	CTRL+LEFT ARROW

Move one word to the right.	CTRL+RIGHT ARROW
Select or cancel selection one character to the left.	SHIFT+LEFT ARROW
Select or cancel selection one character to the right.	SHIFT+RIGHT ARROW
Select or cancel selection one word to the left.	CTRL+SHIFT+LEFT ARROW
Select or cancel selection one word to the right.	CTRL+SHIFT+RIGHT ARROW
Select from the insertion point to the beginning of the entry.	SHIFT+HOME
Select from the insertion point to the end of the entry.	SHIFT+END

CHAPTER 8

Keyboard Shortcuts In SharePoint Workspace (Groove) 2010.

Definition of Program: Microsoft SharePoint Workspace formerly known as Microsoft Groove is a document collaboration in teams with members who are usually offline or who don't share the same network security clearance.

Keyboard shortcuts are designed to work with supported Web browsers. The behavior of keyboard shortcuts differs depending on the browser that you use. For example, in Windows Internet Explorer, the shortcut key combination that is assigned to a hyperlink places the active focus on that hyperlink. You must then press ENTER to follow the hyperlink. In Firefox, pressing the key combination follows the link automatically.

In browsers that do not support shortcut key combinations, you may still be able to use the TAB key to move between commands.

The following keyboard shortcuts will help you become a successful user of Microsoft SharePoint Workspace 2010.

Common Keyboard Shortcuts.

The following keyboard shortcuts apply to items in most tools.

TASK	SHORTCUT
Copy the selected item as a link.	CTRL+L
Copy the selected item to the Clipboard	CTRL+C
Cut the selected item	CTRL+X
Paste from the Clipboard	CTRL+V
Undo the most recent action	CTRL+Z
Redo the most recent action	CTRL+Y
Go to the next item	F8
Go to the previous item	SHIFT+F8
Go to the next unread item.	F4
Go to the previous unread item.	SHIFT+F4
Mark the selected item read (remove unread marker).	CTRL+F4
Mark all items read (remove all unread markers).	CTRL+SHIFT+F4

2010 Documents tool, 2007 Files tool, 2007 SharePoint Files tool

TASK	SHORTCUT
Add an existing document to the workspace.	CTRL+M
Delete a document.	CTRL+D

2010 Discussion Tool.

Keyboard shortcuts for 2010 Discussion tools are exactly the same as those described in the next section for 2010 Lists tool.

2010 Lists Tools.

TASK	SHORTCUT
DELETE the selected item.	CTRL+D
Import data from other sources.	CTRL+I
Export data to a List Data Archive file.	CTRL+E
In a list view, find the next or previous item that contains the specified text. In an open list item, find the specified text.	CTRL+F
In an open list item, find the specified text, and replace it with specified text.	CTRL+H
Enter the Designer to modify forms and views for this list.	CTRL+SHIFT+S

2010 Calendar Tool.

Keyboard shortcuts in a Calendar view

TASK	SHORTCUT
Create a new meeting	ENTER (with no meeting selected) or CTRL+N
Open a selected meeting	ENTER
Save changes in a meeting without closing it	CTRL+S
Display the Month view	CTRL+1
Display the Week view	CTRL+2
Display the Day view	CTRL+3
Display the Work Week view	CTRL+4
Display the Work Month view	CTRL+5

Display all meetings in a list	CTRL+6
Display all active meetings in a list	CTRL+7
Go to a specific date	CTRL+D
Go to today	CTRL+T

Keyboard shortcuts in an open Calendar meeting

TASK	SHORTCUT
Display the meeting profile	CTRL+1
Display the meeting agenda	CTRL+2
Display the meeting notes	CTRL+3
Display the meeting summary	CTRL+4
Delete this meeting	CTRL+D

Notepad Tool

TASK	SHORTCUT
Create a new note	CTRL+N
Save an edited note	CTRL+S
Save and close an edited note	CTRL+W
Cancel edits in a note	ESCAPE
Delete a note	CTRL+DELETE
Edit the selected note	CTRL+E
Move to next note	F8
Move to previous note	SHIFT+F8

Pictures Tool

TASK	SHORTCUT
Add one or more pictures to the list	CTRL+O
Save a picture file to your computer	CTRL+E

Sketchpad Tool

TASK	SHORTCUT
Save text typed in the Type tool to the sketch	CTRL+S
Selection tool	S
Pencil tool	P
Line tool	L
Rectangle tool	R
Rounded Rectangle tool	O
Ellipse tool	E
Polygon tool	G
Text tool	T

2007 Calendar Tool

TASK	SHORTCUT
Create a new appointment	CTRL+N
View details for a selected appointment	ENTER
Go to a specific date	CTRL+D
Go to the next/previous day, week, or month, depending on the Calendar view	PGDN/PGUP
Go to the next/previous appointment	F8/SHIFT+F8
Go to the next/previous unread appointment	F4/SHIFT+F4
Go to the current date according to your computer's system clock	CTRL+T

Messages

TASK	SHORTCUT
Create a new message	CTRL+G
Send a message to all members of a workspace	CTRL+SHIFT+G

Message History

TASK	SHORTCUT
Create a new message	CTRL+N
Open a selected message	CTRL+O
Reply to a selected message	CTRL+R
Forward a selected message	CTRL+W
Delete a selected message	CTRL+D
Find messages	CTRL+F
Print a selected message	CTRL+P
Check/uncheck "Include history in replies"	CTRL+H

CHAPTER 9.

Keyboard Shortcuts For Use In InfoPath 2010.

Definition of Program: Microsoft InfoPath is an electronic Program used to design, fill and submit electronic forms that has to do with structured data. It is a Microsoft Corporation program first released in 2003.

The following keyboard shortcuts will help you become a successful user of Microsoft InfoPath 2010.

Navigating The Ribbon.

Change the focus without using the mouse

TASK	SHORTCUT
Move left or right to another tab of the Ribbon, respectively.	TAB to get to the desired tab, and then LEFT ARROW, RIGHT ARROW
Display the shortcut menu for the selected command.	ENTER
Move the focus to each command on the Ribbon, forward or backward respectively.	TAB, SHIFT+TAB
Move down, up, left, or right among the items on the Ribbon, respectively.	DOWN ARROW, UP ARROW, LEFT ARROW, RIGHT ARROW

Activate the selected command or control on the Ribbon.	SPACE BAR or ENTER
Open the selected menu or gallery on the Ribbon.	SPACE BAR or ENTER
Activate a command or control on the Ribbon so you can modify a value.	ENTER
Finish modifying a value in a control on the Ribbon, and move the focus back to the document.	ENTER

All Pages.

All pages

TASK	SHORTCUT
Turn More Accessible Mode on or off. More Accessible Mode changes the way content is rendered on a site, optimizing it for assistive technologies such as screen readers.	TAB (Press repeatedly, immediately after opening the page in a browser.)
Activate or place focus on the **Skip to main content** link.	ALT+X
Activate or place focus on the **Skip Ribbon Commands** link.	ALT+Y
Activate or place focus on the **View All Site Content** link.	ALT+3
Activate or place focus on the **Site Actions** menu.	ALT+/

Activate or place focus on the **Search** box. Placing focus on the **Search** box requires the ribbon to have the active focus (press ALT+/ to place focus on the **Site Actions** menu, and then press TAB repeatedly until the focus is placed on the **Browse** tab).	ALT+S
Activate or place focus on the **Help** link.	ALT+6
Activate or place focus on the **Home** link.	ALT+1
Activate or place focus on the **Your Name** menu. Press ALT+W multiple times to toggle between the **Your Name** menu and any Web Parts on the page.	ALT+W
Expand menus such as the drop-down menu for a list item.	SHIFT+ENTER
Expand drop down lists such as the **Search Scope** menu next to the **Search** box at the top of some pages.	ALT+DOWN ARROW
Move the selection from Web Part to Web Part on pages that use multiple Web Parts	ALT+W

Common Tasks.

Edit Rich text

Rich text editing is available in several locations, such as the ribbon for a publishing page or the Content Editor Web Part.

TASK	SHORTCUT
Change the text color. This requires the ribbon to have the active focus (Press ALT+/ to place focus on the **Site Actions** menu, and then press TAB repeatedly until you reach the **Format Text** tab under **Editing Tools**).	TAB (Press repeatedly until the **Font Color** menu is selected.)
Change the text size. This requires the ribbon to have the active focus (Press ALT+/ to place focus on the **Site Actions** menu, and then press TAB repeatedly until you reach the **Format Text** tab under **Editing Tools**).	TAB (Press repeatedly until the **Font Size** menu is selected.)
Change the text font. This requires the ribbon to have the active focus (Press ALT+/ to place focus on the **Site Actions** menu, and then press TAB repeatedly until you reach the **Format Text** tab under **Editing Tools**).	TAB (Press repeatedly until the **Font** menu is selected.)

Apply or remove bold formatting from the selected text.	CTRL+B
Apply or remove italic formatting from the selected text.	CTRL+I
Apply or remove the underline from the selected text.	CTRL+U
Change the highlight color of text. This requires the ribbon to have the active focus (Press ALT+/ to place focus on the **Site Actions** menu, and then press TAB repeatedly until you reach the **Format Text** tab under **Editing Tools**).	TAB (Press repeatedly until the **Highlight Color** button is selected.)
Left align the selected paragraph.	CTRL+L
Center the selection.	CTRL+E
Right align the selected paragraph.	CTRL+R
Convert the selection to a left-to-right orientation.	CTRL+SHIFT+ >
Convert the selection to a right-to-left orientation.	CTRL+SHIFT+ <
Create a numbered list. This requires the ribbon to have the active focus (Press ALT+/ to place focus on the **Site Actions** menu, and	TAB (Press repeatedly until the **Numbered List** button is selected.)

then press TAB repeatedly until you reach the **Format Text** tab under **Editing Tools**).	
Apply or remove bulleted list formatting from the selected paragraph. This requires the ribbon to have the active focus (Press ALT+/ to place focus on the **Site Actions** menu, and then press TAB repeatedly until you reach the **Format Text** tab under **Editing Tools**).	TAB (Press repeatedly until the **Bulleted List** button is selected.)
Remove a paragraph indent from the left.	CTRL+SHIFT+M
Indent a paragraph from the left.	CTRL+ M
Delete the selection without placing it on the Clipboard.	DELETE
Switch between inserting and overwriting text.	INSERT
Delete the selection, or if there is no selection, the character preceding the cursor.	BACKSPACE
Delete all of the word preceding the cursor, but not the preceding space.	CTRL+BACKSPACE
Insert a new line (but not inside the HTML Paragraph element <P>).	SHIFT+ENTER

For pages or dialog boxes that have Open or Cancel buttons

To apply or cancel edits in pages or dialog boxes that have Open, Save, Create or Cancel buttons, use the following keyboard shortcuts. Such dialog boxes and pages include such New Alert, Upload Document, or New Library.

TASK	SHORTCUT
Cancel button (cancels changes and returns to the list, library, discussion board, or survey)	ALT+C
Depending on the context, the **OK**, **Save** or **Create** button (saves changes and closes the page or dialog box.)	ALT+O

List or library page

TASK	SHORTCUT
Create a new document.	Press TAB repeatedly until the item that you want is selected. In a library, the ribbon button name may be **New document**. In a list, the ribbon button name may be **New item**, or a name specific to the type of list, such as **Add new link**.
Upload a document. This requires the ribbon to have the active focus (Press ALT+/ to place	Press TAB repeatedly until the link that you want is selected.

focus on the **Site Actions** menu, and then press TAB repeatedly until you reach the ribbon tab that you want).	In a library, the command may be **Add new document** or **Add new item**. In a list, the command may be **Add new item** or specific to the type of list, such as **Add new link**.
Edit a page in datasheet view. This requires the ribbon to have the active focus (Press ALT+/ to place focus on the **Site Actions** menu, and then press TAB repeatedly until you reach the ribbon tab that you want).	TAB (Press repeatedly until **Datasheet View** is selected on the **List** or **Library** tab.)
Open an item with Windows Explorer. This requires the ribbon to have the active focus (Press ALT+/ to place focus on the **Site Actions** menu, and then press TAB repeatedly until you reach the ribbon tab that you want).	TAB (Press repeatedly until **Open with Explorer** is selected on the **List** or **Library** tab.)
Export a list to Microsoft Excel 2010. This requires the ribbon to have the active focus	TAB (Press repeatedly until **Export to Excel** is selected on the **List** or **Library** tab.)

(Press ALT+/ to place focus on the **Site Actions** menu, and then press TAB repeatedly until you reach the ribbon tab that you want).	
View the RSS feed for the library. This requires the ribbon to have the active focus (Press ALT+/ to place focus on the **Site Actions** menu, and then press TAB repeatedly until you reach the ribbon tab that you want).	TAB (Press repeatedly until **RSS Feed** is selected on the **List** or **Library** tab.)
Create an alert for the library. This requires the ribbon to have the active focus (Press ALT+/ to place focus on the **Site Actions** menu, and then press TAB repeatedly until you reach the ribbon tab that you want).	TAB (Press repeatedly until **Alert Me** is selected on the **List** or **Library** tab.)
Create a column. This requires the ribbon to have the active focus (Press ALT+/ to place focus on the **Site Actions** menu, and then press TAB	TAB (Press repeatedly until **Create Column** is selected on the **List** or **Library** tab.)

repeatedly until you reach the ribbon tab that you want).	
Create a view. This requires the ribbon to have the active focus (Press ALT+/ to place focus on the **Site Actions** menu, and then press TAB repeatedly until you reach the ribbon tab that you want).	TAB (Press repeatedly until **Create View** is selected on the **List** or **Library** tab.)
Change the library settings. This requires the ribbon to have the active focus (Press ALT+/ to place focus on the **Site Actions** menu, and then press TAB repeatedly until you reach the ribbon tab that you want).	TAB (Press repeatedly until **Library Settings** is selected on the **List** or **Library** tab.)
Create a folder. This requires the ribbon to have the active focus (Press ALT+/ to place focus on the **Site Actions** menu, and then press TAB repeatedly until you reach the ribbon tab that you want).	TAB (Press repeatedly until **New Folder** is selected on the **List** or **Documents** tab.)

Expand the menu of options for a document in a library. This requires the main content area to have the active focus (Press ALT+X).	TAB (Press repeatedly until the downward pointing arrow on the menu is selected, then press ENTER.)
Filter a column in a list. This requires the main content area to have the active focus (Press ALT+X) to place focus in the main content area, and then press TAB repeatedly)	TAB (Press repeatedly until the downward pointing arrow on the menu is selected, then press ENTER.)

Slide Library Page

TASK	SHORTCUT
Upload slides. This requires the main content area to have the active focus (Press ALT+X).	TAB (Press repeatedly until **Upload** menu selected, then press DOWN ARROW to select **Publish Slides**.)
Delete slides. This command is on the **Actions** menu.	TAB (Press repeatedly until **Actions** menu selected, then press DOWN ARROW to select **Delete**.)
Copy slide to a presentation.	ALT+N

Picture Library Page

TASK	SHORTCUT
Activate or place focus on the **Edit** command. This command is on the **Actions** menu.	ALT+C (To activate the menu, press SHIFT+ENTER. To select a command, press DOWN ARROW.)
Activate or place focus on the **Delete** command. This command is on the **Actions** menu.	ALT+C (To activate the menu, press SHIFT+ENTER. To select a command, press DOWN ARROW.)
Activate or place focus on the **Download** command. This command is on the **Actions** menu.	ALT+C (To activate the menu, press SHIFT+ENTER. To select a command, press DOWN ARROW.)
Activate or place focus on the **Send To** command. This command is on the **Actions** menu.	ALT+C (To activate the menu, press SHIFT+ENTER. To select a command, press DOWN ARROW.)
Activate or place focus on the **View Slide Show** command. This command is on the **Actions** menu.	ALT+C (To activate the menu, press SHIFT+ENTER. To select a command, press DOWN ARROW.)
Activate or place focus on the **Open with Windows Explorer** command.	ALT+C (To activate the menu, press SHIFT+ENTER. To select a command, press DOWN ARROW.)

This command is on the **Actions** menu.	

Survey Page

TASK	SHORTCUT
Activate or place focus on the **Actions** menu.	ALT+C (To activate the menu, press SHIFT+ENTER. To select a command, press DOWN ARROW.)
Activate or place focus on the **Respond to this Survey** button.	ALT+N
Activate or place focus on the **Export Results to spreadsheet** command. This command is on the **Actions** menu.	ALT+C (To activate the menu, press SHIFT+ENTER. To select a command, press DOWN ARROW.)
Activate or place focus on the **Show a graphical summary of responses** link.	ALT+R
In a form for editing a survey response, select the **Save and Close** button.	ALT+S
Activate or place focus on the **Show all responses** link.	ALT+U
Activate or place focus on the **Settings** menu.	ALT+I

Activate or place focus on the **Next Page** button.	ALT+N

Permissions Page

TASK	SHORTCUT
Grant users permissions. This requires the ribbon to have the active focus (Press ALT+/ to place focus on the **Site Actions** menu, and then press TAB repeatedly until you reach the ribbon tab that you want).	TAB (Press repeatedly until you select the **Grant Permissions** button on the **Edit** tab.)
Create a group. This requires the ribbon to have the active focus (Press ALT+/ to place focus on the **Site Actions** menu, and then press TAB repeatedly until you reach the ribbon tab that you want).	TAB (Press repeatedly until you select **Create Group** on the **Edit** tab.)
Remove user permissions. This requires the ribbon to have the active focus (Press ALT+/ to place focus on the **Site Actions** menu, and then press TAB repeatedly until you reach the ribbon tab that you want).	TAB (Press repeatedly until you select **Remove User Permissions** on the **Edit** tab.)
Edit user permissions. This requires the ribbon to have the active focus (Press ALT+/ to	TAB (Press repeatedly until you select **Edit User Permissions** on the **Edit** tab.)

place focus on the **Site Actions** menu, and then press TAB repeatedly until you reach the ribbon tab that you want).	
Check Permissions. This requires the ribbon to have the active focus (Press ALT+/ to place focus on the **Site Actions** menu, and then press TAB repeatedly until you reach the ribbon tab that you want).	TAB (Press repeatedly until you select **Check Permissions** on the **Edit** tab.)

All Site Content page

TASK	SHORTCUT
Activate or place focus on the **Create** link.	ALT+N

Discussion Board

TASK	SHORTCUT
Activate or place focus on the **Add new discussion** link. This requires the main content area to have the active focus (Press ALT+X).	TAB (Press repeatedly until you reach the **Add new discussion** link.)

Calendar view

TASK	SHORTCUT
Activate or place focus on the **Day** view link This requires the ribbon to have the active focus (Press ALT+/ to place focus on the **Site Actions** menu, and then press TAB repeatedly until you reach the ribbon tab that you want).	TAB (Press repeatedly until you select **Day** on the **Calendar** tab.)
Activate or place focus on the **Week** view link This requires the ribbon to have the active focus (Press ALT+/ to place focus on the **Site Actions** menu, and then press TAB repeatedly until you reach the ribbon tab that you want).	TAB (Press repeatedly until you select **Week** on the **Calendar** tab.)
Activate or place focus on the **Month** view link This requires the ribbon to have the active focus (Press ALT+/ to place focus on the **Site Actions** menu, and then press TAB repeatedly until you reach the ribbon tab that you want).	TAB (Press repeatedly until you select **Month** on the **Calendar** tab.)
In a date picker control, move to the previous month	ALT+<
In a date picker control, move to the next month	ALT+>

Web Part Page

TASK	SHORTCUT
Move to the next Web Part.	ALT+W
Open the **Web Part** menu. (This requires that the Web Part have the active focus. Press ALT+X to skip to the main content, then press ALT+W repeatedly until you select the title for the Web Part that you want. Press TAB to select the menu.)	ENTER
Edit a Web Part. (This requires that the **Web Part** menu have the active focus. Press ALT+W repeatedly until you select the title for the Web Part that you want, press TAB, and then press ENTER.)	TAB (Press repeatedly until **Edit Web Part** is selected)
Save property changes in the **Web Part** tool pane, and then close the tool pane.	ALT+O
Save property changes in the **Web Part** tool pane, and keep the tool pane open.	ALT+Y
Cancel property changes in the **Web Part** tool pane, and then close the tool pane.	ALT+C
Add the selected Web Part in the Add Web Parts pane to a Web Part Page.	TAB (Press repeatedly until **Add** is selected)
Move to the previous item in a drop down list, menu, or submenu.	UP ARROW

Move to the next item in a drop down list, menu, or submenu.	DOWN ARROW

Managing Microsoft InfoPath 2010 forms in a Library.

TASK	SHORTCUT
Merge forms This requires the ribbon to have the active focus (Press ALT+/ to place focus on the **Site Actions** menu, and then press TAB repeatedly until you reach the **Library** tab on the ribbon.	Press TAB repeatedly until the **Current View** menu is selected, and then press DOWN ARROW several times to select **Merge Documents**.
Edit a form in Microsoft InfoPath 2010 This requires the main content area to have the active focus (Press ALT+X).	TAB (Press repeatedly until the downward pointing arrow on the menu for the form is selected. Press ENTER, and then press DOWN ARROW to select **Edit in Microsoft InfoPath**.)
Edit a form in the browser This requires the main content area to have the active focus (Press ALT+X).	TAB (Press repeatedly until the downward pointing arrow on the menu for the form is selected. Press ENTER, and then press DOWN ARROW to select **Edit in Browser**.)
Create a new form in a library	Press TAB repeatedly until **New Document** is selected.

| This requires the ribbon to have the active focus (Press ALT+/ to place focus on the **Site Actions** menu, and then press TAB repeatedly until you reach the **Documents** tab on the ribbon. | |

Use the keyboard to work with the ribbon

Do tasks quickly without using the mouse by pressing a few keys—no matter where you are in an Office program. You can get to every command on the ribbon by using an access key—usually by pressing two to four keys.

1. Press and release the ALT key.
2. You see the little boxes called KeyTips over each command available in the current view.
3. Press the letter shown in the KeyTip over the command you want to use.
4. Depending on which letter you pressed, you might see additional KeyTips. For example, if the **Home** tab is active and you pressed N, the **Insert** tab is displayed, along with the KeyTips for the groups in that tab.
5. Continue pressing letters until you press the letter of the specific command you want to use.

Tip: To cancel the action you're taking and hide the KeyTips, press and release the ALT key.

Change the keyboard focus without using the mouse

Another way to use the keyboard to work with the ribbon is to move the focus among the tabs and commands until you find the feature you want to use. The following shows some ways to move the keyboard focus without using the mouse.

TASK	SHORTCUT
Select the active tab and show the access keys.	ALT or F10. Press either of these keys again to move back to the Office file and cancel the access keys.
Move to another tab.	ALT or F10 to select the active tab, and then LEFT ARROW or RIGHT ARROW.
Move to another Group on the active tab.	ALT or F10 to select the active tab, and then CTRL+RIGHT ARROW or LEFT ARROW to move between groups.
Minimize (collapse) or restore the ribbon.	CTRL+F1
Display the shortcut menu for the selected item.	SHIFT+F10
Move the focus to select the active tab, your Office file, task pane, or status bar.	F6
Move the focus to each command in the ribbon, forward or backward.	ALT or F10, and then TAB or SHIFT+TAB
Move down, up, left, or right among the items in the ribbon.	DOWN ARROW, UP ARROW, LEFT ARROW, or RIGHT ARROW

Go to the selected command or control in the ribbon.	SPACE BAR or ENTER
Open the selected menu or gallery in the ribbon.	SPACE BAR or ENTER
Go to a command or option in the ribbon so you can change it.	ENTER
Finish changing the value of a command or option in the ribbon, and move focus back to the Office file.	ENTER
Get help on the selected command or control in the ribbon. (If no Help article is associated with the selected command, the Help table of contents for that program is shown instead.)	F1

Getting Help.

Using the Help window

The Help window provides access to all Help content for a SharePoint site. The Help window displays topics and other Help content.

In the Help window

TASK	SHORTCUT
Open the Help window.	ALT+6
Close the Help window.	ALT+F4

Switch between the Help window and the active program.	ALT+TAB
Perform the default action for the selected item.	ENTER
In the Help and how-to window, select the next or previous item, respectively.	TAB or SHIFT+TAB
In the Help topic, expand or collapse the selected item, respectively.	ENTER
Select the next hidden text or hyperlink, including **Show All** or **Hide All** at the top of a topic.	TAB
Select the previous hidden text or hyperlink.	SHIFT+TAB
Perform the action for the selected **Show All**, **Hide All**, hidden text, or hyperlink.	ENTER
Move back to the previous Help topic (**Back** button).	ALT+LEFT ARROW or BACKSPACE
Move forward to the next Help topic (**Forward** button).	ALT+RIGHT ARROW
Scroll small amounts up or down, respectively, within the currently displayed Help topic.	UP ARROW, DOWN ARROW
Scroll larger amounts up or down, respectively, within the currently displayed Help topic.	PAGE UP, PAGE DOWN
Stop the last action (**Stop** button).	ESC
Refresh the window (**Refresh** button).	F5
Print the current Help topic.	CTRL+P

Note: If the current Help topic is not the active window, press ALT+F6, and then press CTRL+P.	
Type text in the search box.	TAB (Press repeatedly)
Select the previous hyperlink.	SHIFT+TAB
Print the current Help topic.	CTRL+P

Navigating SharePoint 2010 sites that do not have UI upgrades applied

All pages

TASK	SHORTCUT
Turn More Accessible Mode on or off. More Accessible Mode changes the way content is rendered on a Office SharePoint Server 2007 or Office Forms Server 2007 site, optimizing it for assistive technologies such as screen readers.	TAB (Press repeatedly, immediately after opening the page in a browser.)
Activate or place focus on the **Skip to main content** link.	ALT+J
Activate or place focus on the **View All Site Content** link.	ALT+3
Activate or place focus on the **Site Actions** menu.	ALT+/
Activate or place focus on the **Search** link.	ALT+S
Activate or place focus on the **Help** link.	ALT+6

Activate or place focus on the **Home** link.	ALT+1
Activate or place focus on the **Welcome** menu.	ALT+L
Activate or place focus on the **View** menu.	ALT+V
Expand menus such as the **Site Actions** menu.	SHIFT+ENTER
Expand drop down lists such as the **Search Scope** menu next to the **Search** box at the top of most pages.	ALT+DOWN ARROW
Move the selection from Web Part to Web Part on pages, such as on the home page, that use multiple Web Parts.	ALT+W

Rich Text Editing

TASK	SHORTCUT
Activate or place focus on the **Right-to-Left text direction** button.	CTRL+SHIFT+<
Activate or place focus on the **Left-to-Right text direction** button.	CTRL+SHIFT+>
Activate or place focus on the **Bold** button.	CTRL+B
Activate or place focus on the **Copy** button.	CTRL+C
Activate or place focus on the **Text color** button.	CTRL+SHIFT+C
Activate or place focus on the **Center** button.	CTRL+E
Activate or place focus on the **Numbered List** button.	CTRL+SHIFT+E

Activate or place focus on the **Font** menu.	CTRL+SHIFT+F
Activate or place focus on the **Italics** button.	CTRL+I
Activate or place focus on the **Align Left** button.	CTRL+L
Activate or place focus on the **Bulleted List** button.	CTRL+SHIFT+L
Activate or place focus on the **Increase Indent** button.	CTRL+M
Activate or place focus on the **Decrease Indent** button.	CTRL+SHIFT+M
Activate or place focus on the **Font Size** menu.	CTRL+SHIFT+P
Activate or place focus on the **Align Right** button.	CTRL+R
Activate or place focus on the **Underline** button.	CTRL+U
Activate or place focus on the **Paste** button.	CTRL+V
Activate or place focus on the **Background Color** menu.	CTRL+SHIFT+W
Activate or place focus on the **Cut** button.	CTRL+X

Add or Edit Item, Document, Discussion Comment, or Survey Response

TASK	SHORTCUT
Cancel button (cancels changes and returns to the list, library, discussion board, or survey)	ALT+C
OK button (saves changes and closes the page)	ALT+O

List or Library Page

TASK	SHORTCUT
Activate or place focus on the **New** menu on a list or library toolbar.	ALT+N (To activate the menu, press SHIFT+ENTER. To select a command, press DOWN ARROW.)
Activate or place focus on the **Upload** menu on a list or library toolbar. Depending on the type of library, the **Upload** menu contains **Upload Document** and **Upload Multiple Document** commands.	ALT+U (To activate the menu, press SHIFT+ENTER. To select a command, press DOWN ARROW.)
Activate or place focus on the **Actions** menu on a list or library toolbar. Depending on the type of list or library, the **Actions** menu contains **Edit in Datasheet**, **Open with Windows Explorer**, **Export to Spreadsheet**, **View RSS Feed**, and **Alert Me** commands.	ALT+C (To activate the menu, press SHIFT+ENTER. To select a command, press DOWN ARROW.)
Activate or place focus on the **Settings** menu on a list or library toolbar. Depending on the type of list or library, the **Settings** menu	ALT+I (To activate the menu, press SHIFT+ENTER. To select a command, press DOWN ARROW.)

contains **Create Column**, **Create View**, and **Library Type Library Settings** commands.	
Create **New Document** This command is on the **New** menu.	ALT+N (To activate the menu, press SHIFT+ENTER. To select a command, press DOWN ARROW.)
Create **New Folder** This command is on the **New** menu.	ALT+N (To activate the menu, press SHIFT+ENTER. To select a command, press DOWN ARROW.)
Upload Document This command is on the **Upload** menu.	ALT+U (To activate the menu, press SHIFT+ENTER. To select a command, press DOWN ARROW.)
In a standard view, **Edit in Datasheet** This command is on the **Actions** menu.	ALT+C (To activate the menu, press SHIFT+ENTER. To select a command, press DOWN ARROW.)
Expand the menu of options for a document in a library.	SHIFT+ENTER
Filter a column in a list. This requires that the column header have the active focus (press ALT+J to skip to the main content area, and then press TAB repeatedly until the header is selected).	SHIFT+ENTER

Picture Library Page

TASK	SHORTCUT
Edit This command is on the **Actions** menu.	ALT+C (To activate the menu, press SHIFT+ENTER. To select a command, press DOWN ARROW.)
Delete This command is on the **Actions** menu.	ALT+C (To activate the menu, press SHIFT+ENTER. To select a command, press DOWN ARROW.)
Download This command is on the **Actions** menu.	ALT+C (To activate the menu, press SHIFT+ENTER. To select a command, press DOWN ARROW.)
Send To This command is on the **Actions** menu.	ALT+C (To activate the menu, press SHIFT+ENTER. To select a command, press DOWN ARROW.)
View Slide Show This command is on the **Actions** menu.	ALT+C (To activate the menu, press SHIFT+ENTER. To select a command, press DOWN ARROW.)
Open with Windows Explorer	ALT+C (To activate the menu, press SHIFT+ENTER. To select a command, press DOWN ARROW.)

This command is on the **Actions** menu.	

Survey Page

TASK	SHORTCUT
Activate or place focus on the **Actions** menu.	ALT+C (To activate the menu, press SHIFT+ENTER. To select a command, press DOWN ARROW.)
Activate or place focus on the **Respond to this Survey** button.	ALT+N
Export Results to spreadsheet This command is on the **Actions** menu.	ALT+C (To activate the menu, press SHIFT+ENTER. To select a command, press DOWN ARROW.)
Show a graphical summary of responses link.	ALT+R
In a form for editing a survey response, select the **Save and Close** button.	ALT+S
Activate or place focus on the **Show all responses** link.	ALT+U
Activate or place focus on the **Settings** menu.	ALT+I
Activate or place focus on the **Next Page** button.	ALT+N

Nanci

Permissions Page

TASK	SHORTCUT
Remove User Permissions This command is on the **Actions** menu.	ALT+C (To activate the menu, press SHIFT+ENTER. To select a command, press DOWN ARROW.)
Edit User Permissions This command is on the **Actions** menu.	ALT+C (To activate the menu, press SHIFT+ENTER. To select a command, press DOWN ARROW.)
Inherit Permissions This command is on the **Actions** menu.	ALT+C (To activate the menu, press SHIFT+ENTER. To select a command, press DOWN ARROW.)

All Site Content page

TASK	SHORTCUT
Activate or place focus on the **Create** button.	ALT+N

Discussion board

TASK	SHORTCUT
Activate or place focus on the **New Discussion** button.	ALT+N

Calendar view

TASK	SHORTCUT
Activate or place focus on the **Day** view link.	ALT+PERIOD
Activate or place focus on the **Week** view link.	ALT+MINUS SIGN
Activate or place focus on the **Month** view link.	ALT+EQUAL SIGN
Move to the previous day, week, or month in a view.	ALT+[
Move to the next day, week, or month in a view.	ALT+]
In a date picker control, move to the previous month.	ALT+<
In a date picker control, move to the next month.	ALT+>

Contacts list

TASK	SHORTCUT
Connect to Outlook This command is on the **Actions** menu.	ALT+C (To activate the menu, press SHIFT+ENTER. To select a command, press DOWN ARROW.)

Web Part Page

TASK	SHORTCUT
Move to the next Web Part or tool pane section.	ALT+W
Open the **Web Part** menu. (This requires that the Web Part have the	ALT+ENTER

active focus. Press ALT+W repeatedly until you select the title for the Web Part that you want, and then press the TAB key.)	
Modify a Web Part. (This requires that the **Web Part** menu have the active focus. Press ALT+W repeatedly until you select the title for the Web Part that you want, press the TAB key, and then press ALT+ENTER.)	DOWN ARROW (press repeatedly)
Save property changes in the **Web Part** tool pane, and then close the tool pane.	ALT+O
Save property changes in the **Web Part** tool pane, and keep the tool pane open.	ALT+Y
Cancel property changes in the **Web Part** tool pane, and then close the tool pane.	ALT+C
Add the selected Web Part in the Add Web Parts window to a Web Part Page.	ALT+O
Move to the previous item in a drop down list, menu, or submenu.	UP ARROW
Move to the next item in a drop down list, menu, or submenu.	DOWN ARROW
Close a submenu and return to the previous menu or submenu.	LEFT ARROW
Open the next submenu.	RIGHT ARROW

Rich Text Editor of the Content Editor Web Part.

The following keyboard shortcuts apply to the Content Editor Web Part.

The Standard Toolbar

TASK	SHORTCUT
Cut the selection to the Clipboard.	CTRL+X
Copy the selection to the Clipboard.	CTRL+C
Paste the contents of the Clipboard to the current location.	CTRL+V SHIFT+INSERT
Undo the most recent command.	CTRL+Z
Redo the most recently undone command.	CTRL+Y
Find text.	CTRL+F
Switch between hiding and showing gridlines.	CTRL+SHIFT+G
Create a hyperlink for a selection or edit an existing hyperlink.	CTRL+L
Insert an image.	ALT+CTRL+I
Insert a table.	ALT+SHIFT+T
Insert a row in a table.	ALT+CTRL+R
Insert a column in a table.	ALT+CTRL+C
Insert a cell in a table.	ALT+CTRL+L
Merge cells in a table.	ALT+CTRL+M
Split cells in a table.	ALT+CTRL+S
Get help.	F1

The Formatting Toolbar

TASK	SHORTCUT
Change the text style.	CTRL+SHIFT+S
Change the text font.	CTRL+SHIFT+F
Apply or remove bold formatting from the selected text.	CTRL+B

Apply or remove italic formatting from the selected text.	CTRL+I
Apply or remove the underline from the selected text.	CTRL+U
Change the background color of text.	CTRL+SHIFT+B
Left align the selected paragraph.	ALT+SHIFT+[
Center the selection.	ALT+SHIFT+|
Right align the selected paragraph.	ALT+SHIFT+]
Convert the selection to a left-to-right orientation.	CTRL+SHIFT+ >
Convert the selection to a right-to-left orientation.	CTRL+SHIFT+ <
Create a numbered list.	ALT+CTRL+N
Apply or remove bulleted list formatting from the selected paragraph.	ALT+CTRL+B
Remove a paragraph indent from the left.	CTRL+SHIFT+T
Indent a paragraph from the left.	CTRL+T

Editing Content

TASK	SHORTCUT
Delete the selection without placing it on the Clipboard.	DELETE
Switch between inserting and overwriting text.	INSERT
Delete the selection, or if there is no selection, the character preceding the cursor.	BACKSPACE
Delete all of the word preceding the cursor, but not the preceding space.	CTRL+BACKSPACE

Insert a new line (but not inside an HTML Paragraph element: <P>).	SHIFT+ENTER

Navigating Content

TASK	SHORTCUT
Move the cursor one character to the right.	RIGHT ARROW
Move the cursor one character to the left.	LEFT ARROW
Move the cursor up one line.	UP ARROW
Move the cursor down one line.	DOWN ARROW
Move the cursor forward one word.	CTRL+RIGHT ARROW
Move the cursor back one word.	CTRL+LEFT ARROW
Move the cursor to the start of the line.	HOME
Move the cursor to the end of the line.	END
Move the cursor up one paragraph.	CTRL+UP ARROW
Move the cursor down one paragraph.	CTRL+DOWN ARROW
Move the cursor up one page.	PAGE UP
Move the cursor down one page.	PAGE DOWN
Move the cursor to the beginning of the content.	CTRL+HOME
Move the cursor to the end of the content.	CTRL+END

Extending The Selection Of Content

TASK	SHORTCUT
Extend the selection one character to the right.	SHIFT+RIGHT ARROW
Extend the selection one character to the left.	SHIFT+LEFT ARROW
Extend the selection one word to the right.	CTRL+SHIFT+RIGHT ARROW
Extend the selection one word to the left.	CTRL+SHIFT+LEFT ARROW
Extend the selection up one line.	SHIFT+UP ARROW
Extend the selection down one line.	SHIFT+DOWN ARROW
Extend the selection to the end of the line.	SHIFT+END
Extend the selection to the start of the line.	SHIFT+HOME
Extend the selection up one page.	SHIFT+PAGE UP
Extend the selection down one page.	SHIFT+PAGE DOWN
Extend the selection to the beginning of the content.	CTRL+SHIFT+HOME
Extend the selection to the end of the content.	CTRL+SHIFT+END
Select the entire content.	CTRL+A

Navigating tables, images, or objects (HTML block elements)

TASK	SHORTCUT
Move to the next table, image, or object (HTML block element) in the content.	TAB
Move to the previous table, image, or object (HTML block element) in the content.	SHIFT+TAB
Move from the content to the next block element on the Web page.	CTRL+TAB
Move to the **Save** button.	SHIFT+CTRL+TAB
Switch between absolute and relative positioning for the table, image, or object (HTML block element).	CTRL+K

Managing Microsoft InfoPath 2010 forms in a library.

TASK	SHORTCUT
Merge Documents. This command is on the **View** menu.	ALT+W (To activate the menu, press SHIFT+ENTER.)
Edit in Microsoft Office InfoPath. This requires the menu of options for a form to have the active focus (press ALT+J to skip to the main content area, and then press TAB repeatedly until	SHIFT+ENTER

the menu of options is displayed).	
Edit in Browser This requires the menu of options for a form to have the active focus (press ALT+J to skip to the main content area, and then press TAB repeatedly until the menu of options is displayed).	SHIFT+F10, DOWN ARROW (press four times)
Create a new form in a library (**New Document**). This command is on the **New** menu.	ALT+N (To activate the menu, press SHIFT+ENTER.)

CHAPTER 10

Keyboard Shortcuts In Project 2010.

Definition of Program: Microsoft Project is a project management software, developed and sold by Microsoft that helps users to create schedules, distribute resources and manage budgets.

The following keyboard shortcuts will help you become a successful user of Microsoft Project 2010.

Online Help

Use the Help window

The Help window provides access to all Office Help content. The Help window displays topics and other Help content.

In The Help Window.

TASK	SHORTCUT
Open the Help window.	F1
Close the Help window.	ALT+F4
Switch between the Help window and the active program.	ALT+TAB
Go back to **Program Name** Home.	ALT+HOME
Select the next item in the Help window.	TAB
Select the previous item in the Help window.	SHIFT+TAB

Perform the action for the selected item.	ENTER
In the **Browse Program Name Help** section of the Help window, select the next or previous item, respectively.	TAB or SHIFT+TAB
In the **Browse Program Name Help** section of the Help window, expand or collapse the selected item.	ENTER
Select the next hidden text or hyperlink, including **Show All** or **Hide All** at the top of a topic.	TAB
Select the previous hidden text or hyperlink.	SHIFT+TAB
Perform the action for the selected **Show All**, **Hide All**, hidden text, or hyperlink.	ENTER
Move back to the previous Help topic (**Back** button).	ALT+LEFT ARROW or BACKSPACE
Move forward to the next Help topic (**Forward** button).	ALT+RIGHT ARROW
Scroll small amounts up or down, respectively, within the currently displayed Help topic.	UP ARROW or DOWN ARROW
Scroll larger amounts up or down, respectively, within the currently displayed Help topic.	PAGE UP or PAGE DOWN
Change whether the Help window appears connected to (tiled) or separate from (untiled) the active program.	ALT+U
Display a menu of commands for the Help window. This requires that the	SHIFT+F10

Help window have the active focus (click in the Help window).	
Stop the last action (**Stop** button).	ESC
Update the window (**Refresh** button).	F5
Print the current Help topic. **Note:** If the cursor is not in the current Help topic, press F6 and then press CTRL+P.	CTRL+P
Change the connection state.	F6, DOWN ARROW
Type text in the **Type words to search for** box.	F6, DOWN ARROW
Switch among areas in the Help window; for example, switch between the toolbar, **Type words to search for** box, and **Search** list.	F6
In a Table of Contents in tree view, select the next or previous item, respectively.	DOWN ARROW or UP ARROW
In a Table of Contents in tree view, expand or collapse the selected item, respectively.	LEFT ARROW or RIGHT ARROW

Microsoft Office Basics.

Keyboard access to the Office Fluent Ribbon

1. Press ALT.

   The KeyTips are displayed over each feature that is available in the current view.

2. Press the letter that appears in the KeyTip over the feature that you want to use.
3. Depending on which letter you press, additional KeyTips may appear. For example, if the **Home** tab is active and you press W, the **View** tab is displayed, along with the KeyTips for the groups on that tab.
4. Continue pressing letters until you press the letter of the command or control that you want to use. In some cases, you must first press the letter of the group that contains the command.

Note: To cancel the action that you are taking and hide the KeyTips, press ALT.

Tip: If the Watch Window does not get focus after you select it by using the KeyTips, press ALT, and then press CTRL+TAB.

Display And Use Windows.

TASK	SHORTCUT
Switch to the next window.	ALT+TAB
Switch to the previous window.	ALT+SHIFT+TAB
Close the active window.	CTRL+W or CTRL+F4
Restore the size of the active window after you maximize it.	CTRL+F5
Move to a task pane from another pane in the program window (clockwise direction). You may need to press F6 more than once. **Note:** If pressing F6 doesn't display the task pane you want, try pressing ALT to place focus on the menu bar	F6

or Ribbon, which is a part of the Office Fluent Ribbon, and then pressing CTRL+TAB to move to the task pane.	
Move to a pane from another pane in the program window (counterclockwise direction).	SHIFT+F6
When more than one window is open, switch to the next window.	CTRL+F6
Switch to the previous window.	CTRL+SHIFT+F6
When a document window is not maximized, perform the **Move** command (on the **Control** menu for the window). Press the arrow keys to move the window. When you finish, press ESC.	CTRL+F7
When a document window is not maximized, perform the **Size** command (on the **Control** menu for the window). Press the arrow keys to resize the window. When you finish, press ESC.	CTRL+F8
Minimize a window to an icon (works for only some Microsoft Office programs).	CTRL+F9
Maximize or restore a selected window.	CTRL+F10
Copy a picture of the screen to the Clipboard.	PRINT SCREEN
Copy a picture of the selected window to the Clipboard.	ALT+PRINT SCREEN

Change or Resize the Font

TASK	SHORTCUT
Change the font.	CTRL+SHIFT+F
Change the font size.	CTRL+SHIFT+P
Increase the font size of the selected text.	CTRL+SHIFT+>
Decrease the font size of the selected text.	CTRL+SHIFT+<

Move Around in Text or Cells

TASK	SHORTCUT
Move one character to the left.	LEFT ARROW
Move one character to the right.	RIGHT ARROW
Move one line up.	UP ARROW
Move one line down.	DOWN ARROW
Move one word to the left.	CTRL+LEFT ARROW
Move one word to the right.	CTRL+RIGHT ARROW
Move to the end of a line.	END
Move to the beginning of a line.	HOME
Move up one paragraph.	CTRL+UP ARROW
Move down one paragraph.	CTRL+DOWN ARROW
Move to the end of a text box.	CTRL+END
Move to the beginning of a text box.	CTRL+HOME
Repeat the last **Find** action.	SHIFT+F4

Move Around in and Work in Tables

TASK	SHORTCUT
Move to the next cell.	TAB
Move to the preceding cell.	SHIFT+TAB

Move to the next row.	DOWN ARROW
Move to the preceding row.	UP ARROW
Insert a tab in a cell.	CTRL+TAB
Start a new paragraph.	ENTER
Add a new row at the bottom of the table.	TAB at the end of the last row

Access and Use Actions

TASK	SHORTCUT
Display the menu or message for an action. If more than one action is present, switch to the next action and display its menu or message.	ALT+SHIFT+F10
Select the next item on the action menu.	DOWN ARROW
Select the previous item on the action menu.	UP ARROW
Perform the action for the selected item on the action menu.	ENTER
Close the action menu or message.	ESC

Tips

- You can ask to be notified by a sound whenever an action appears. To hear audio cues, you must have a sound card. You must also have Microsoft Office Sounds installed on your computer.
- If you have access to the World Wide Web, you can download Microsoft Office Sounds from the Microsoft Office.com Web site.

Use Dialog Boxes

TASK	SHORTCUT
Move to the next option or option group.	TAB
Move to the previous option or option group.	SHIFT+TAB
Switch to the next tab in a dialog box.	CTRL+TAB
Switch to the previous tab in a dialog box.	CTRL+SHIFT+TAB
Move between options in an open drop-down list, or between options in a group of options.	Arrow keys
Perform the action assigned to the selected button; select or clear the selected check box.	SPACEBAR
Open the list if it is closed and move to that option in the list.	First letter of an option in a drop-down list
Select an option; select or clear a check box.	ALT+ the letter underlined in an option
Open a selected drop-down list.	ALT+DOWN ARROW
Close a selected drop-down list; cancel a command and close a dialog box.	ESC
Perform the action assigned to a default button in a dialog box.	ENTER

Use Edit Boxes Within Dialog Boxes

An edit box is a blank in which you type or paste an entry, such as your user name or the path to a folder.

TASK	SHORTCUT
Move to the beginning of the entry.	HOME
Move to the end of the entry.	END
Move one character to the left or right, respectively.	LEFT ARROW or RIGHT ARROW
Move one word to the left.	CTRL+LEFT ARROW
Move one word to the right.	CTRL+RIGHT ARROW
Select or cancel selection one character to the left.	SHIFT+LEFT ARROW
Select or cancel selection one character to the right.	SHIFT+RIGHT ARROW
Select or cancel selection one word to the left.	CTRL+SHIFT+LEFT ARROW
Select or cancel selection one word to the right.	CTRL+SHIFT+RIGHT ARROW
Select from the insertion point to the beginning of the entry.	SHIFT+HOME
Select from the insertion point to the end of the entry.	SHIFT+END

Use the Open and Save As Dialog Boxes

TASK	SHORTCUT
Go to the previous folder.	ALT+1
Open the folder one level above the open folder.	ALT+2

Close the dialog box and open your Web search page.	ALT+3
Delete the selected folder or file.	ALT+3
Create a new folder.	ALT+4
Switch among available folder views.	ALT+5
Show the **Tools** menu.	ALT+L
Display a shortcut menu for a selected item, such as a folder or file.	SHIFT+F10
Move between options or areas in the dialog box.	TAB
Open the list.	F4 or ALT+I
Update the file list.	F5

Microsoft Project 2010

Use the Network Diagram view

TASK	SHORTCUT
Move to a different Network Diagram box.	Arrow keys
Add Network Diagram boxes to the selection.	SHIFT+Arrow keys
Move a Network Diagram box. **Note:** Manual positioning must be set first. Select the box you want to move. On the **Format** tab, click **Layout** in the **Format** group. Click **Allow manual box positioning**.	CTRL+Arrow keys

Move to the top Network Diagram box in the view or project.	CTRL+HOME or SHIFT+CTRL+HOME
Move to the lowest Network Diagram box in the project.	CTRL+END or SHIFT+CTRL+END
Move to the leftmost Network Diagram box in the project.	HOME or SHIFT+HOME
Move to the rightmost Network Diagram box in the project.	END or SHIFT+END
Move up one window height.	PAGE UP or SHIFT+PAGE UP
Move down one window height.	PAGE DOWN or SHIFT+PAGE DOWN
Move left one window width.	CTRL+PAGE UP or SHIFT+CTRL+PAGE UP
Move right one window width.	CTRL+PAGE DOWN or SHIFT+CTRL+PAGE DOWN
Select the next field in the Network Diagram box.	ENTER or TAB
Select the previous field in the Network Diagram box.	SHIFT+ENTER

Navigate Views and Windows

TASK	SHORTCUT
Activate the **Control** menu.	ALT+SPACEBAR
Activate the entry bar to edit text in a field.	F2
Activate the menu bar.	F10 or ALT
Activate the project control menu.	ALT+HYPHEN

Activate the split bar.	SHIFT+F6
Close the program window.	ALT+F4
Display all filtered tasks or all filtered resources.	F3
Display the **Field Settings** dialog box.	ALT+F3
Open a new window.	SHIFT+F11
Reduce a selection to a single field.	SHIFT+BACKSPACE
Reset sort order to ID order and turn off grouping.	SHIFT+F3
Select a drawing object.	F6
Display task information.	SHIFT+F2
Display resource information.	SHIFT+F2
Display assignment information.	SHIFT+F2
Turn on or off the Add To Selection mode.	SHIFT+F8
Turn on or off Auto Calculate.	CTRL+F9
Turn on or off the Extend Selection mode.	F8
Move left, right, up, or down to view different pages in the Print Preview window.	ALT+Arrow keys

Outline A Project

TASK	SHORTCUT
Hide subtasks.	ALT+SHIFT+HYPHEN or ALT+SHIFT+MINUS SIGN (minus sign on the numeric keypad)
Indent the selected task.	ALT+SHIFT+RIGHT ARROW
Show subtasks.	ALT+SHIFT+ = or ALT+SHIFT+PLUS SIGN (plus sign on the numeric keypad)

Show all tasks.	ALT+SHIFT+* (asterisk on the numeric keypad)
Outdent the selected task.	ALT+SHIFT+LEFT ARROW

Select and Edit in a Dialog Box

TASK	SHORTCUT
Move between fields at the bottom of a form.	Arrow keys
Move into tables at the bottom of a form.	ALT+1 (left) or ALT+2 (right)
Move to the next task or resource.	ENTER
Move to the previous task or resource.	SHIFT+ENTER

Select and Edit in a Sheet View

Edit in a View

TASK	SHORTCUT
Cancel an entry.	ESC
Clear or reset the selected field.	CTRL+DELETE
Copy the selected data.	CTRL+C
Cut the selected data.	CTRL+X
Delete the selected data.	DELETE
Delete row that has a selected cell.	CTRL+MINUS SIGN (on the numeric keypad)
Fill down.	CTRL+D
Display the **Find** dialog box.	CTRL+F or SHIFT+F5

In the **Find** dialog box, continue to the next instance of the search results.	SHIFT+F4
Use the **Go To** command (**Edit** menu).	F5
Link tasks.	CTRL+F2
Paste the copied or cut data.	CTRL+V
Reduce the selection to one field.	SHIFT+BACKSPACE
Undo the last action.	CTRL+Z
Unlink tasks.	CTRL+SHIFT+F2
Set the task to manually schedule	CTRL+SHIFT+M
Set the task to auto schedule	CTRL+SHIFT+A

Move in a View

TASK	SHORTCUT
Move to the beginning of a project (timescale).	ALT+HOME
Move to the end of a project (timescale).	ALT+END
Move the timescale left.	ALT+LEFT ARROW
Move the timescale right.	ALT+RIGHT ARROW
Move to the first field in a row.	HOME or CTRL+LEFT ARROW
Move to the first row.	CTRL+UP ARROW
Move to the first field of the first row.	CTRL+HOME
Move to the last field in a row.	END or CTRL+RIGHT ARROW

Move to the last field of the last row.	CTRL+END
Move to the last row.	CTRL+DOWN ARROW

Move in the Side Pane

TASK	SHORTCUT
Move focus between the side pane and the view on the right side.	CTRL+TAB or CTRL+SHIFT+TAB
Select different controls in the side pane if focus is in the side pane.	TAB
Select or clear check boxes and option buttons if focus is in the side pane.	SPACEBAR

Select in a View

TASK	SHORTCUT
Extend the selection down one page.	SHIFT+PAGE DOWN
Extend the selection up one page.	SHIFT+PAGE UP
Extend the selection down one row.	SHIFT+DOWN ARROW
Extend the selection up one row.	SHIFT+UP ARROW
Extend the selection to the first field in a row.	SHIFT+HOME
Extend the selection to the last field in a row.	SHIFT+END
Extend the selection to the start of the information.	CTRL+SHIFT+HOME

Extend the selection to the end of the information.	CTRL+SHIFT+END
Extend the selection to the first row.	CTRL+SHIFT+UP ARROW
Extend the selection to the last row.	CTRL+SHIFT+DOWN ARROW
Extend the selection to the first field of the first row.	CTRL+SHIFT+HOME
Extend the selection to the last field of the last row.	CTRL+SHIFT+END
Select all rows and columns.	CTRL+SHIFT+SPACEBAR
Select a column.	CTRL+SPACEBAR
Select a row.	SHIFT+SPACEBAR
Move within a selection down one field.	ENTER
Move within a selection up one field.	SHIFT+ENTER
Move within a selection right one field.	TAB
Move within a selection left one field.	SHIFT+TAB

Select and Edit in the Entry Bar

TASK	SHORTCUT
Accept an entry.	ENTER
Cancel an entry.	ESC
Delete one character to the left.	BACKSPACE
Delete one character to the right.	DELETE

Delete one word to the right.	CTRL+DELETE
Extend the selection to the end of the text.	SHIFT+END
Extend the selection to the start of the text.	SHIFT+HOME
Turn on or off Overtype mode.	INSERT

Use a Timescale

TASK	SHORTCUT
Move the timescale left one page.	ALT+PAGE UP
Move the timescale right one page.	ALT+PAGE DOWN
Move the timescale to beginning of the project.	ALT+HOME
Move the timescale to end of the project.	ALT+END
Scroll the timescale left.	ALT+LEFT ARROW
Scroll the timescale right.	ALT+RIGHT ARROW
Show smaller time units.	CTRL+ / (slash on the numeric keypad)
Show larger time units.	CTRL+* (asterisk on the numeric keypad)

Note: You can use the keyboard to access commands on the Ribbon, and to navigate to and move around in the Help window. Press ALT to display KeyTips over each feature that is available in the current view.

Use the keyboard to work with the ribbon

Do tasks quickly without using the mouse by pressing a few keys—no matter where you are in an Office program. You can get to every command on the ribbon by using an access key—usually by pressing two to four keys.

1. Press and release the ALT key.
2. You see the little boxes called KeyTips over each command available in the current view.
3. Press the letter shown in the KeyTip over the command you want to use.
4. Depending on which letter you pressed, you might see additional KeyTips. For example, if the **Home** tab is active and you pressed N, the **Insert** tab is displayed, along with the KeyTips for the groups in that tab.
5. Continue pressing letters until you press the letter of the specific command you want to use.

Tip: To cancel the action you're taking and hide the KeyTips, press and release the ALT key.

Change the keyboard focus without using the mouse

Another way to use the keyboard to work with the ribbon is to move the focus among the tabs and commands until you find the feature you want to use. The following shows some ways to move the keyboard focus without using the mouse.

TASK	SHORTCUT
Select the active tab and show the access keys.	ALT or F10. Press either of these keys again to move back to the Office

	file and cancel the access keys.
Move to another tab.	ALT or F10 to select the active tab, and then LEFT ARROW or RIGHT ARROW.
Move to another Group on the active tab.	ALT or F10 to select the active tab, and then CTRL+RIGHT ARROW or LEFT ARROW to move between groups.
Minimize (collapse) or restore the ribbon.	CTRL+F1
Display the shortcut menu for the selected item.	SHIFT+F10
Move the focus to select the active tab, your Office file, task pane, or status bar.	F6
Move the focus to each command in the ribbon, forward or backward.	ALT or F10, and then TAB or SHIFT+TAB
Move down, up, left, or right among the items in the ribbon.	DOWN ARROW, UP ARROW, LEFT ARROW, or RIGHT ARROW
Go to the selected command or control in the ribbon.	SPACE BAR or ENTER
Open the selected menu or gallery in the ribbon.	SPACE BAR or ENTER
Go to a command or option in the ribbon so you can change it.	ENTER
Finish changing the value of a command or option in the	ENTER

ribbon, and move focus back to the Office file.	
Get help on the selected command or control in the ribbon. (If no Help article is associated with the selected command, the Help table of contents for that program is shown instead.)	F1

CHAPTER 11

Keyboard Shortcuts In Visio 2010.

Definition of Program: Microsoft Visio is a diagramming and vector graphics application that was acquired by Microsoft in 2000. With Microsoft Visio, diagrams can be created with just a few clicks.

The following keyboard shortcuts will help you become a successful user of Microsoft Visio 2010.

Online Help

Keyboard shortcuts for using the Help window

The Help window provides access to all Office Help content. The Help window displays topics and other Help content.

In The Help Window.

TASK	SHORTCUT
Open the Help window.	F1
Close the Help window.	ALT+F4
Switch between the Help window and the active program.	ALT+TAB
Go back to Microsoft Visio 2010 Home.	ALT+HOME
Select the next item in the Help window.	TAB

Select the previous item in the Help window.	SHIFT+TAB
Perform the action for the selected item.	ENTER
Select the next hidden text or hyperlink, including **Show All** or **Hide All** at the top of a topic.	TAB
Select the previous hidden text or hyperlink.	SHIFT+TAB
Perform the action for the selected **Show All**, **Hide All**, hidden text, or hyperlink.	ENTER
Move back to the previous Help topic (**Back** button).	ALT+LEFT ARROW
Move forward to the next Help topic (**Forward** button).	ALT+RIGHT ARROW
Scroll small amounts up or down, respectively, within the currently displayed Help topic.	UP ARROW or DOWN ARROW
Scroll larger amounts up or down, respectively, within the currently displayed Help topic.	PAGE UP or PAGE DOWN
Display a menu of commands for the Help window. This requires that the Help window have the active focus (click in the Help window).	SHIFT+F10
Stop the last action (**Stop** button).	ESC
Refresh the window (**Refresh** button).	F5
Switch among areas in the Help window; for example, switch between the toolbar, address bar, and **Search** list.	F6

| In a Table of Contents in tree view, select the next or previous item, respectively. | UP ARROW or DOWN ARROW |
| In a Table of Contents in tree view, expand or collapse the selected item, respectively. | LEFT ARROW or RIGHT ARROW |

Microsoft Office Basics.

Display and Use Windows

TASK	SHORTCUT
Switch to the next window.	ALT+TAB
Switch to the previous window.	ALT+SHIFT+TAB
Close the active window.	ALT+F4
Move to a task pane from another pane in the program window (clockwise direction). You may need to press F6 more than once. **Note:** If pressing F6 does not display the task pane you want, try pressing ALT to put focus on the ribbon.	F6
Maximize a selected window.	CTRL+F10
Restore the size of the Visio program window after you maximized it.	CTRL+F5
Copy a picture of the screen to the Clipboard.	PRINT SCREEN
Copy a picture of the selected window to the Clipboard.	ALT+PRINT SCREEN
For any window with an icon in its title bar (for example, a	ALT+SPACEBAR

shapes window), display the window shortcut menu.	
Open the **Page** dialog box.	SHIFT+F4
Open the **Reorder Pages** dialog box.	CTRL+ALT+P
Cycle the focus through open drawings.	CTRL+TAB or CTRL+F6
Cycle the focus through open drawings in reverse order.	CTRL+SHIFT+TAB or CTRL+SHIFT+F6
Cycle the focus through pages in a drawing, including any visible markup overlays.	CTRL+PAGE DOWN
Cycle the focus through pages in a drawing in reverse order.	CTRL+PAGE UP
When a task pane is active, select the next or previous option in the task pane.	TAB or SHIFT+TAB

Change or resize the font

TASK	SHORTCUT
Increase the font size of the selected text.	CTRL+SHIFT+>
Decrease the font size of the selected text.	CTRL+SHIFT+<

Move around in text or cells

TASK	SHORTCUT
Move one character to the left.	LEFT ARROW
Move one character to the right.	RIGHT ARROW
Move one line up.	UP ARROW
Move one line down.	DOWN ARROW
Move one word to the left.	CTRL+LEFT ARROW

Move one word to the right.	CTRL+RIGHT ARROW
Move to the end of a line.	END
Move to the beginning of a line.	HOME
Move up one paragraph.	CTRL+UP ARROW
Move down one paragraph.	CTRL+DOWN ARROW
Move to the end of a text box.	CTRL+END
Move to the beginning of a text box.	CTRL+HOME

Access and Use Task Panes

TASK	SHORTCUT
Move to a task pane from another pane in the program window. (You may need to press F6 more than once.) **Note:** If pressing F6 does not display the task pane you want, try pressing ALT to put the focus on the ribbon and then pressing F6 to move to the task pane.	F6
When a task pane is active, select the next or previous option in the task pane.	TAB or SHIFT+TAB
Move among choices on a selected submenu; move among certain options in a group of options in a dialog box.	DOWN ARROW or UP ARROW
Open the selected menu, or perform the action assigned to the selected button.	SPACEBAR or ENTER
Open a shortcut menu	SHIFT+F10

When a menu or submenu is visible, select the first or last command, respectively, on the menu or submenu.	HOME or END

Float or Anchor Task Panes

1. Press F6 repeatedly to select the task pane that you want.
2. Press ALT+SPACEBAR to open the menu for that task pane.
3. Press the DOWN ARROW key to select the **Float Window** command, and then press ENTER.

Use Dialog Boxes

TASK	SHORTCUT
Move to the next option or option group.	TAB
Move to the previous option or option group.	SHIFT+TAB
Switch to the next tab in a dialog box.	CTRL+TAB
Switch to the previous tab in a dialog box.	CTRL+SHIFT+TAB
Move between options in an open drop-down list, or between options in a group of options.	Arrow keys
Perform the action assigned to the selected button; select or clear the selected check box.	SPACEBAR

Open the list if it is closed and move to that option in the list.	First letter of an option in a drop-down list
Select an option; select or clear a check box.	ALT+ the letter underlined in an option
Open a selected drop-down list.	ALT+DOWN ARROW
Close a selected drop-down list; cancel a command and close a dialog box.	ESC
Perform the action assigned to a default button in a dialog box.	ENTER

Use edit boxes within dialog boxes

An edit box is a blank in which you type or paste an entry, such as your user name or the path of a folder.

TASK	SHORTCUT
Move to the beginning of the entry.	HOME
Move to the end of the entry.	END
Move one character to the left or right.	LEFT ARROW or RIGHT ARROW
Move one word to the left.	CTRL+LEFT ARROW
Move one word to the right.	CTRL+RIGHT ARROW
Select or cancel selection one character to the left.	SHIFT+LEFT ARROW
Select or cancel selection one character to the right.	SHIFT+RIGHT ARROW
Select or cancel selection one word to the left.	CTRL+SHIFT+LEFT ARROW

Select or cancel selection one word to the right.	CTRL+SHIFT+RIGHT ARROW
Select from the insertion point to the beginning of the entry.	SHIFT+HOME
Select from the insertion point to the end of the entry.	SHIFT+END

Use the Open and Save As dialog boxes

TASK	SHORTCUT
Move to the next option or option group.	TAB
Move to the previous option or option group.	SHIFT+TAB
Move between options in an open drop-down list, or between options in a group of options.	Arrow keys
Perform the action assigned to the selected button	ENTER, SPACEBAR
Move to the **Save as type** list in the **Save As** dialog box	ALT+T
Move to the **File name** box	ALT+N
Move to the file type list in the **Open** dialog box	ALT+T
Open a selected file in the **Open** dialog box	ALT+O
Save the current file in the **Save** dialog box	ALT+S
Open a selected drop-down list.	ALT+DOWN ARROW
Close a selected drop-down list; cancel a command and close a dialog box.	ESC

Update the file list	F5
Display a shortcut menu for a selected item such as a folder or file	SHIFT+F10

Text.

Edit Text

TASK	SHORTCUT
Move to the next or previous character, respectively, in a line of text.	RIGHT ARROW or LEFT ARROW
Move to the next or previous line of text, respectively.	DOWN ARROW or UP ARROW
Move to the next or previous word, respectively, in a line of text.	CTRL+RIGHT ARROW or CTRL+LEFT ARROW
Move to the next or previous paragraph, respectively.	CTRL+DOWN ARROW or CTRL+UP ARROW
Select all the text in a text block.	CTRL+A
Select the next or previous character, respectively.	SHIFT+RIGHT ARROW or SHIFT+LEFT ARROW
Select the next or previous word, respectively.	CTRL+SHIFT+RIGHT ARROW or CTRL+SHIFT+LEFT ARROW
Select the next or previous line, respectively.	SHIFT+DOWN ARROW or SHIFT+UP ARROW

Select the next or previous paragraph, respectively.	CTRL+SHIFT+DOWN ARROW or CTRL+SHIFT+UP ARROW
Delete the previous word.	CTRL+BACKSPACE
Replace the selected text with the field height. If no text is selected, replace all text with the field height for the selected shape.	CTRL+SHIFT+H

Format Text

TASK	SHORTCUT
Turn bold (**B**) on or off.	CTRL+B
Turn italic (*I*) on or off.	CTRL+I
Turn underline (U) on or off.	CTRL+U
Turn double underline on or off.	CTRL+SHIFT+D
Turn all caps on or off.	CTRL+SHIFT+A
Turn small caps on or off.	CTRL+SHIFT+K
Turn subscript (x_2) on or off.	CTRL+=
Turn superscript (x^2) on or off.	CTRL+SHIFT+=
Increase the font size of the selected text.	CTRL+SHIFT+>
Decrease the font size of the selected text.	CTRL+SHIFT+<

Align Text

TASK	SHORTCUT
Align text left.	CTRL+SHIFT+L
Center text horizontally.	CTRL+SHIFT+C
Align text right.	CTRL+SHIFT+R
Justify text horizontally.	CTRL+SHIFT+J
Top-align text vertically.	CTRL+SHIFT+T

Center text vertically.	CTRL+SHIFT+M
Bottom-align text vertically.	CTRL+SHIFT+V

Zoom And Navigation.

Navigate the Ribbon

1. Press ALT.

   The KeyTips are displayed over each feature that is available in the current view.

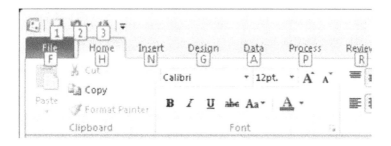

2. Press the letter shown in the KeyTip over the feature that you want to use.
3. Depending on which letter you press, you may be shown additional KeyTips. For example, if the **Home** tab is active and you press N, the **Insert** tab is displayed, along with the KeyTips for the groups on that tab.
4. Continue pressing letters until you press the letter of the command or control that you want to use. In some cases, you must first press the letter of the group that contains the command. For example, if the **Home** tab is active, press ALT+H, F, S will take you to the **Size** list box in the **Font** group.

   Note: To cancel the action that you are taking and hide the KeyTips, press ALT.

Zoom

TASK	SHORTCUT
Zoom in.	ALT+F6
Zoom out.	ALT+SHIFT+F6
Fit to window	CTRL+SHIFT+W

Move around in full-screen view

Use these keyboard shortcuts to move between Visio and another program or page when you are in full-screen view.

TASK	SHORTCUT
Enter full-screen view	F5
Exit full-screen view	ESC
Open the next page in the drawing.	PAGE DOWN
Return to the previous page in the drawing.	PAGE UP

Move around a Web page drawing

TASK	SHORTCUT
Cycle the focus through the left frame, the drawing, and shapes on the drawing that contain shape data, hyperlinks, and the address bar.	TAB
Activate the hyperlink for the shape or hyperlink on the drawing that has focus.	ENTER

Visio-Specific Tasks.

Format text

TASK	SHORTCUT
Open the **Home** tab in the ribbon	ALT+H

Open the **Font** tab in the **Text** dialog box.	F11
Open the **Paragraph** tab in the **Text** dialog box.	SHIFT+F11
Open the **Tabs** tab in the **Text** dialog box.	CTRL+F11
Open the **Fill** dialog box for the selected shape.	F3
Open the **Line** dialog box.	SHIFT+F3

Use the Snap & Glue features

TASK	SHORTCUT
Open the **General** tab in the **Snap & Glue** dialog box.	ALT+F9
Select or clear the **Snap** check box on the **General** tab in the **Snap & Glue** dialog box; snaps shapes to items selected in the **Snap to** section of the dialog box.	S
Select or clear the **Glue** check box on the **General** tab in the **Snap & Glue** dialog box; glues shapes to items selected in the **Glue to** section of the dialog box (**Tools** menu, **Snap & Glue**).	G

Group, rotate, and flip shapes

TASK	SHORTCUT
Group the selected shapes.	CTRL+G or CTRL+SHIFT+G
Ungroup shapes in the selected group.	CTRL+SHIFT+U
Bring the selected shape to the front.	CTRL+SHIFT+F

Send the selected shape to the back.	CTRL+SHIFT+B
Rotate the selected shape to the left.	CTRL+L
Rotate the selected shape to the right.	CTRL+R
Flip the selected shape horizontally.	CTRL+H
Flip the selected shape vertically.	CTRL+J
Open the **Align Shapes** dialog box for the selected shape.	F8

View drawing windows

TASK	SHORTCUT
Display the open drawing windows tiled vertically.	SHIFT+F7
Display the open drawing windows tiled horizontally.	CTRL+SHIFT+F7
Display the open drawing windows so that you can see the title of every window.	ALT+F7 or CTRL+ALT+F7

Visio-Specific Toolbars.

Select tools

TASK	SHORTCUT
Switch the **Format Painter** tool on or off ( ).	CTRL+SHIFT+P
Select the **Pointer Tool** ( ).	CTRL+1
Select the **Connector** tool ( ).	CTRL+3
Select the connection point tool	CTRL+SHIFT+1

Select the text tool (A).	CTRL+2
Select the text box tool (⚉).	CTRL+SHIFT+4

Select the drawing tools

TASK	SHORTCUT
Select the **Rectangle Tool** (□).	CTRL+8
Select the **Ellipse Tool** (○).	CTRL+9
Select the **Line Tool** (╱).	CTRL+6
Select the **Arc Tool** (◠).	CTRL+7
Select the **Freeform Tool** (∿).	CTRL+5
Select the **Pencil Tool** (✎).	CTRL+4

Crop a picture

TASK	SHORTCUT
Select the **Crop** tool (⌗).	CTRL+SHIFT+2

Visio Shapes And Stencils.

Move from shape to shape in a drawing page

TASK	SHORTCUT
Move from shape to shape on the drawing page. A dotted rectangle indicates the shape that has the focus. **Note:** You cannot move to shapes that are protected against selection or on a locked layer.	TAB
Move from shape to shape on the drawing page in reverse order.	SHIFT+TAB
Select a shape that has focus.	ENTER

Note: To select multiple shapes, press the TAB key to bring focus to the first shape you want to select, and then press ENTER. Hold down SHIFT while you press the TAB key to bring focus to another shape. When the focus rectangle is over the shape you want, press ENTER to add that shape to the selection. Repeat for each shape you want to select.	
Clear selection of or focus on a shape.	ESC
Switch between text edit mode and shape selection mode on a selected shape.	F2
Nudge a selected shape.	Arrow keys
Nudge a selected shape 1 pixel at a time. **Note:** SCROLL LOCK must be turned off.	SHIFT+Arrow keys

Work with master shapes in a stencil

TASK	SHORTCUT
Move between master shapes in a stencil.	Arrow keys
Move to the first master shape in a row of a stencil.	HOME
Move to the last master shape in a row of a stencil.	END
Move to the first master shape in a column of a stencil.	PAGE UP
Move to the last master shape in a column of a stencil.	PAGE DOWN
Copy the selected master shapes to the Clipboard.	CTRL+C

Paste the contents of the Clipboard to a new stencil. **Note:** The new stencil must first be opened for editing.	CTRL+V
Select all the master shapes in a stencil. **Note:** To select multiple master shapes, press the arrow keys to bring focus to the first master shape you want. Hold down SHIFT while you press the arrow keys to bring focus to another master. When the focus rectangle is over the master you want, press ENTER to add that master to the selection. Repeat for each master you want to select.	CTRL+A
Select or cancel selection of a master shape that has focus.	SHIFT+ENTER
Cancel the selection of master shapes in a stencil.	ESC
Insert the selected master shapes into the drawing.	CTRL+ENTER

Work with stencils in edit mode

TASK	SHORTCUT
Delete the selected master shape.	DELETE
Cut the selected master shape from the custom stencil and put it on the Clipboard.	CTRL+X
Rename the selected master shape.	F2

CHAPTER 12

Keyboard Shortcuts For Use In Publisher 2010.

Definition of Program: Microsoft Publisher is a Microsoft Office Program designed in 1991 for Desktop Publishing. It is included in Office 2010 bundle.

The following keyboard shortcuts will help you become a successful user of Microsoft Publisher 2010.

Online Help.

Keyboard shortcuts for using the Help window

The Help window provides access to all Office Help content. The Help window displays topics and other Help content.

In The Help Window.

TASK	SHORTCUT
Open the Help window.	F1
Close the Help window	ALT+F4
Switch between the Help window and the active program.	ALT+TAB
Go back to **Program Name** Home.	ALT+HOME
Select the next item in the Help window.	TAB

Select the previous item in the Help window.	SHIFT+TAB
Perform the action for the selected item.	ENTER
In the **Browse Program Name Help** section of the Help window, select the next or previous item, respectively.	TAB or SHIFT+TAB
In the **Browse Program Name Help** section of the Help window, expand or collapse the selected item, respectively.	ENTER
Select the next hidden text or hyperlink, including **Show All** or **Hide All** at the top of a topic.	TAB
Select the previous hidden text or hyperlink.	SHIFT+TAB
Perform the action for the selected **Show All**, **Hide All**, hidden text, or hyperlink.	ENTER
Move back to the previous Help topic (**Back** button).	ALT+LEFT ARROW or BACKSPACE
Move forward to the next Help topic (**Forward** button).	ALT+RIGHT ARROW
Scroll small amounts up or down, respectively, within the currently displayed Help topic.	UP ARROW, DOWN ARROW
Scroll larger amounts up or down, respectively, within the currently displayed Help topic.	PAGE UP, PAGE DOWN
Change whether the Help window appears connected to (tiled) or	ALT+U

separate from (untiled) the active program.	
Display a menu of commands for the Help window. This requires that the Help window have the active focus (click in the Help window).	SHIFT+F10
Stop the last action (**Stop** button).	ESC
Refresh the window (**Refresh** button).	F5
Print the current Help topic. **Note:** If the cursor is not in the current Help topic, press F6 and then press CTRL+P.	CTRL+P
Change the connection state.	F6, and then click DOWN ARROW
Type text in the **Type words to search for** box.	F6, and then click DOWN ARROW
Switch among areas in the Help window; for example, switch between the toolbar, **Type words to search for** box, and **Search** list.	F6
In a Table of Contents in tree view, select the next or previous item, respectively.	UP ARROW, DOWN ARROW
In a Table of Contents in tree view, expand or collapse the selected item, respectively.	LEFT ARROW, RIGHT ARROW

Microsoft Office Basics.

Display and use windows

TASK	SHORTCUT
Switch to the next window.	ALT+TAB

Switch to the previous window.	ALT+SHIFT+TAB
Close the active window.	CTRL+W or CTRL+F4
Restore the size of the active window after you maximize it.	CTRL+F5
Move to a task pane from another pane in the program window (clockwise direction). You may need to press F6 more than once. **Note:** If pressing F6 doesn't display the task pane you want, try pressing ALT to place focus on the menu bar or Ribbon, which is a part of the Microsoft Office Fluent user interface, and then pressing CTRL+TAB to move to the task pane.	F6
Move to a pane from another pane in the program window (counterclockwise direction).	SHIFT+F6
When more than one window is open, switch to the next window.	CTRL+F6
Switch to the previous window.	CTRL+SHIFT+F6
When a document window is not maximized, perform the **Move** command (on the **Control** menu for the window). Use the arrow keys to move the window, and, when finished, press ESC.	CTRL+F7
When a document window is not maximized, perform the **Size** command (on the **Control** menu for the window). Press the arrow	CTRL+F8

keys to resize the window, and, when finished, press ESC.	
Minimize a window to an icon (works for only some Microsoft Office programs).	CTRL+F9
Maximize or restore a selected window.	CTRL+F10
Copy a picture of the screen to the Clipboard.	PRINT SCREEN
Copy a picture of the selected window to the Clipboard.	ALT+PRINT SCREEN

Change or resize the font

TASK	SHORTCUT
Change the font	CTRL+SHIFT+F
Change the font size	CTRL+SHIFT+P
Increase the font size of the selected text	CTRL+SHIFT+>
Decrease the font size of the selected text	CTRL+SHIFT+<

Move around in text or cells

TASK	SHORTCUT
Move one character to the left.	LEFT ARROW
Move one character to the right.	RIGHT ARROW
Move one line up.	UP ARROW
Move one line down.	DOWN ARROW
Move one word to the left.	CTRL+LEFT ARROW
Move one word to the right.	CTRL+RIGHT ARROW
Move to the end of a line.	END
Move to the beginning of a line.	HOME
Move up one paragraph.	CTRL+UP ARROW

Move down one paragraph.	CTRL+DOWN ARROW
Move to the end of a text box.	CTRL+END
Move to the beginning of a text box.	CTRL+HOME
Repeat the last **Find** action.	SHIFT+F4

Move around in and work in tables

TASK	SHORTCUT
Move to the next cell.	TAB
Move to the preceding cell.	SHIFT+TAB
Move to the next row.	DOWN ARROW
Move to the preceding row.	UP ARROW
Insert a tab in a cell.	CTRL+TAB
Start a new paragraph.	ENTER
Add a new row at the bottom of the table.	TAB at the end of the last row

Access and use task panes

TASK	SHORTCUT
Move to a task pane from another pane in the program window. (You may need to press F6 more than once.) **Note:** If pressing F6 doesn't display the task pane you want, try pressing ALT to place focus on the menu bar and then pressing CTRL+TAB to move to the task pane.	F6
When a menu or toolbar is active, move to a task pane. (You may need	CTRL+TAB

to press CTRL+TAB more than once.)	
When a task pane is active, select the next or previous option in the task pane.	TAB or SHIFT+TAB
Display the full set of commands on the task pane menu.	CTRL+DOWN ARROW
Move among choices on a selected submenu; move among certain options in a group of options in a dialog box.	DOWN ARROW or UP ARROW
Open the selected menu, or perform the action assigned to the selected button.	SPACEBAR or ENTER
Open a shortcut menu; open a drop-down menu for the selected gallery item.	SHIFT+F10
When a menu or submenu is visible, select the first or last command on the menu or submenu.	HOME or END
Scroll up or down in the selected gallery list.	PAGE UP or PAGE DOWN
Move to the top or bottom of the selected gallery list.	CTRL+HOME or CTRL+END
Open the Research task pane. **Note:** This keyboard shortcut does not work in Microsoft Office PowerPoint or Microsoft Office SharePoint Designer.	ALT+Click

Access and use smart tags

TASK	SHORTCUT
Display the menu or message for a smart tag. If more than one smart tag is present, switch to the next smart tag and display its menu or message.	ALT+SHIFT+F10
Select the next item on a smart tag menu.	DOWN ARROW
Select the previous item on a smart tag menu.	UP ARROW
Perform the action for the selected item on a smart tag menu.	ENTER
Close the smart tag menu or message.	ESC

Tip: You can ask to be notified by a sound whenever a smart tag appears. To hear audio cues, you must have a sound card. You must also have Microsoft Office Sounds installed on your computer.

Resize and move toolbars, menus, and task panes

1. Press ALT to select the menu bar.
2. Press CTRL+TAB repeatedly to select the toolbar or task pane that you want.
3. Do one of the following:

   ### Resize a toolbar

   a. On the toolbar, press CTRL+SPACEBAR to display the **Toolbar Options** menu.
   b. Click the **Size** command, and then press ENTER.

c. Use the arrow keys to resize the toolbar. Press CTRL+ the arrow keys to resize one pixel at a time.

Move a toolbar

d. On the toolbar, press CTRL+SPACEBAR to display the **Toolbar Options** menu.
e. Click the **Move** command, and then press ENTER.
f. Use the arrow keys to position the toolbar. Press CTRL+ the arrow keys to move one pixel at a time. To undock the toolbar, press DOWN ARROW repeatedly. To dock the toolbar vertically on the left or right side, press LEFT ARROW or RIGHT ARROW, respectively, when the toolbar is all the way to the left or right side.

Resize a task pane

g. In the task pane, press CTRL+SPACEBAR to display a menu of additional commands.
h. Use the DOWN ARROW key to select the **Size** command, and then press ENTER.
i. Use the arrow keys to resize the task pane. Use CTRL+ the arrow keys to resize one pixel at a time.

Move a task pane

j. In the task pane, press CTRL+SPACEBAR to display a menu of additional commands.
k. Use the DOWN ARROW key to select the **Move** command, and then press ENTER.

l. Use the arrow keys to position the task pane. Use CTRL+ the arrow keys to move one pixel at a time.

4. When you finish moving or resizing, press ESC.

Use Dialog Boxes

TASK	SHORTCUT
Move to the next option or option group.	TAB
Move to the previous option or option group.	SHIFT+TAB
Switch to the next tab in a dialog box.	CTRL+TAB
Switch to the previous tab in a dialog box.	CTRL+SHIFT+TAB
Move between options in an open drop-down list, or between options in a group of options.	Arrow keys
Perform the action assigned to the selected button; select or clear the selected check box.	SPACEBAR
Open the list if it is closed and move to that option in the list.	First letter of an option in a drop-down list
Select an option; select or clear a check box.	ALT+ the letter underlined in an option
Open a selected drop-down list.	ALT+DOWN ARROW

Close a selected drop-down list; cancel a command and close a dialog box.	ESC
Perform the action assigned to a default button in a dialog box.	ENTER

Use edit boxes within dialog boxes

An edit box is a blank in which you type or paste an entry, such as your user name or the path to a folder.

TASK	SHORTCUT
Move to the beginning of the entry.	HOME
Move to the end of the entry.	END
Move one character to the left or right.	LEFT ARROW or RIGHT ARROW
Move one word to the left.	CTRL+LEFT ARROW
Move one word to the right.	CTRL+RIGHT ARROW
Select or cancel selection one character to the left.	SHIFT+LEFT ARROW
Select or cancel selection one character to the right.	SHIFT+RIGHT ARROW
Select or cancel selection one word to the left.	CTRL+SHIFT+LEFT ARROW
Select or cancel selection one word to the right.	CTRL+SHIFT+RIGHT ARROW
Select from the insertion point to the beginning of the entry.	SHIFT+HOME

Select from the insertion point to the end of the entry.	SHIFT+END

Use the Open Publication and Save As dialog boxes

TASK	SHORTCUT
Go to the previous folder.	ALT+1
Up One Level button: open the folder up one level above the open folder.	ALT+2
Search the Web button: close the dialog box and open your Web search page	ALT+3
Delete button: delete the selected folder or file.	ALT+3
Create New Folder button: create a new folder.	ALT+4
Views button: switch among available folder views.	ALT+5
Tools button: show the **Tools** menu.	ALT+L
Display a shortcut menu for a selected item such as a folder or file.	SHIFT+F10
Move between options or areas in the dialog box.	TAB
Open the **Look in** list.	F4 or ALT+I
Refresh the file list.	F5

Create, Open, Close, Or Save A Publication.

Create, open, close a publication

TASK	SHORTCUT
Open a new instance of Publisher.	CTRL+N
Display the **Open Publication** dialog box.	CTRL+O
Close the current publication.	CTRL+F4 or CTRL+W
Display the **Save As** dialog box.	CTRL+S

Edit Or Format Text Or Objects.

Edit or format text

Most of these keyboard shortcuts do not work if you are viewing the publication in Web Page Preview.

TASK	SHORTCUT
Display the **Find and Replace** task pane, with the **Find** option selected under **Find or Replace**. These keyboard shortcuts might not work if another task pane is already open. This keyboard shortcut does work in Web Page Preview.	F3 or CTRL+F or SHIFT+F4
Display the **Find and Replace** task pane, with the **Replace** option selected under **Find or**	CTRL+H

Replace. These keyboard shortcuts might not work if another task pane is already open.	
Check spelling.	F7
Display the **Research** task pane to find synonyms.	SHIFT+F7
Display the **Research** task pane to perform a query.	Hold down ALT and click a word
Select all the text. If the cursor is in a text box, this keyboard shortcut selects all text in the current story. If the cursor is not in any text box, this keyboard shortcut selects all the objects on a page.	CTRL+A
Make text bold.	CTRL+B
Italicize text.	CTRL+I
Underline text.	CTRL+U
Make text small capital letters, or return small capital letters to upper and lower case.	CTRL+SHIFT+K
Select the **Style** box on the **Formatting** toolbar.	CTRL+SHIFT+S
Select the **Font** box on the **Formatting** toolbar.	CTRL+SHIFT+F
Select the **Font Size** box on the **Formatting** toolbar.	CTRL+SHIFT+P
Copy formatting.	CTRL+SHIFT+C
Paste formatting.	CTRL+SHIFT+V
Turn **Special Characters** on or off.	CTRL+SHIFT+Y
Return character formatting to the current text style.	CTRL+SPACEBAR

Apply or remove subscript formatting.	CTRL+=
Apply or remove superscript formatting.	CTRL+SHIFT+=
Increase space between letters in a word (kerning).	CTRL+SHIFT+]
Decrease space between letters in a word (kerning).	CTRL+SHIFT+[
Increase font size by 1.0 point.	CTRL+]
Decrease font size by 1.0 point.	CTRL+[
Increase to the next size in the **Font Size** box.	CTRL+SHIFT+>
Decrease to the next size in the **Font Size** box.	CTRL+SHIFT+<
Set center alignment for a paragraph.	CTRL+E
Set left alignment for a paragraph.	CTRL+L
Set right alignment for a paragraph.	CTRL+R
Set justified alignment for a paragraph.	CTRL+J
Set distributed alignment for a paragraph.	CTRL+SHIFT+D
Set newspaper alignment for a paragraph (East Asian languages only).	CTRL+SHIFT+J
Display the **Hyphenation** dialog box. This keyboard shortcut does not work for Web pages.	CTRL+SHIFT+H
Insert the current time.	ALT+SHIFT+T
Insert the current date.	ALT+SHIFT+D
Insert the current page number.	ALT+SHIFT+P
Insert a zero-width non-breaking space.	CTRL+SHIFT+0 (zero)

Set the current paragraph to single spacing.	CTRL+1
Set the current paragraph to double spacing.	CTRL+2
Set the current paragraph to 1.5-line spacing.	CTRL+5

Copy text formats

TASK	SHORTCUT
Copy formatting from text.	CTRL+SHIFT+C
Apply copied formatting to text.	CTRL+SHIFT+V

Copy, cut, paste or delete text or objects

TASK	SHORTCUT
Copy the selected text or object.	CTRL+C or CTRL+INSERT
Cut the selected text or object.	CTRL+X or SHIFT+DELETE
Paste text or an object.	CTRL+V or SHIFT+INSERT
Delete the selected object.	DELETE or CTRL+SHIFT+X

Undo or redo an action

TASK	SHORTCUT
Undo the last action.	CTRL+Z or ALT+BACKSPACE
Redo the last action.	CTRL+Y or F4

Nudge an object

TASK	SHORTCUT

Nudge a selected object up, down, left, or right.	Arrow keys
If the selected object has a cursor in its text, nudge the selected object up, down, left, or right.	ALT+arrow keys

Layer objects

TASK	SHORTCUT
Bring object to front.	ALT+F6
Send object to back.	ALT+SHIFT+F6

Snap objects

TASK	SHORTCUT
Turn **Snap to Guides** on or off.	CTRL+SHIFT+W
Turn **Snap to Guides** on or off	F10, SHIFT+R, SHIFT+S, SHIFT+M
Turn **Snap to Guides** on or off	F10, SHIFT+R, SHIFT+S, SHIFT+O

Select or Group Objects

TASK	SHORTCUT
Select all objects on the page — if your cursor is not in text in a text box or AutoShape. If your cursor is in a text box and you press these keystrokes, this selects all the text that is in a story — even if the story flows to additional text boxes.	CTRL+A

Group selected objects, or ungroup grouped objects.	CTRL+SHIFT+G
Clears the selection from text — if text is selected — but the object that contains the text remains selected.	ESC
Clears the selection from an object — if an object is selected.	ESC
Selects the object within the group — if that object contains text that is already selected.	ESC

Make an object transparent

TASK	SHORTCUT
Switch between making an object transparent or opaque (with a white fill).	CTRL+T

Insert An Object

To use this keyboard shortcut, you must first select the **Objects Toolbar** or the **Insert** menu.

To use this keyboard shortcut from the **Objects Toolbar**, first press ALT to select the menu bar, and then press CTRL+TAB until the **Objects Toolbar** is selected. Then press TAB or SHIFT+TAB to select the button for the type of object you want to insert in your publication.

To use this shortcut key from the **Insert** menu, first press ALT+I, and then use the DOWN ARROW key to select the menu item for the type of object you want to insert.

TASK	SHORTCUT
Insert a text box, line, connector, circle, or square that is selected on the	CTRL+ENTER

Objects Toolbar or **Insert** menu. Alternatively, open a menu or dialog box that provides more options for inserting another type of object.	

Work With Pages.

Select or insert pages

If your publication is in Two-Page Spread view, these commands apply to the selected two-page spread. If your publication is not in Two-Page Spread view, these commands apply only to the selected page.

TASK	SHORTCUT
Display the **Go To Page** dialog box.	F5 or CTRL+G
Insert a page or a two-page spread. If you are creating a newsletter, it opens the **Insert publication type Pages** dialog box. If you are creating a greeting card or program, a message displays asking if you want multiple pages automatically inserted.	CTRL+SHIFT+N
Insert duplicate page after the selected page.	CTRL+SHIFT+U

Move between pages

TASK	SHORTCUT
Display the **Go To Page** dialog box.	F5 or CTRL+G
Go to the next page.	CTRL+PAGE DOWN
Go to the previous page.	CTRL+PAGE UP

Switch between the current page and the master page.	CTRL+M

Use the master page

TASK	SHORTCUT
Switch between the current page and the master page.	CTRL+M

Show or hide boundaries or guides

TASK	SHORTCUT
Turn **Boundaries and Guides** on or off.	CTRL+SHIFT+O
Turn **Horizontal Baseline Guides** on or off. This keyboard shortcut is not available in Web view.	CTRL+F7
Turn **Vertical Baseline Guides** on or off (East Asian languages only). This keyboard shortcut is not available in Web view.	CTRL+SHIFT+F7

Zoom

TASK	SHORTCUT
Switch between the current view and the actual size.	F9
Zoom to full page view.	CTRL+SHIFT+L

Print A Publication.

Use Print Preview

These keyboard shortcuts are available when you are in Print Preview (**File** menu, **Print Preview** command).

TASK	SHORTCUT
Switch between the current view and the actual size.	F9
Scroll up or down.	UP ARROW or DOWN ARROW
Scroll left or right.	LEFT ARROW or RIGHT ARROW
Scroll up in large increments.	PAGE UP or CTRL+UP ARROW
Scroll down in large increments.	PAGE DOWN or CTRL+DOWN ARROW
Scroll left in large increments.	CTRL+LEFT ARROW
Scroll right in large increments.	CTRL+RIGHT ARROW
Scroll to the upper left corner of the page.	HOME
Scroll to the lower right corner of the page.	END
Display the **Go To Page** dialog box.	F5 or CTRL+G
Go to the previous page.	CTRL+PAGE UP
Go to the next page.	CTRL+PAGE DOWN
Go to the next window if you have multiple publications open on your desktop.	CTRL+F6
Exit Print Preview and display the **Print** dialog box.	CTRL+P
Exit Print Preview.	ESC

Print a publication

TASK	SHORTCUT
Open the **Print** dialog box.	CTRL+P

Work With Web Pages And E-Mail.

Insert hyperlinks and preview Web pages

TASK	SHORTCUT
Display the **Insert Hyperlink** dialog box. Your cursor must first be in a text box.	CTRL+K
Preview your Web page in an instance of your browser.	CTRL+SHIFT+B

Send e-mail

After you choose **Send as Message** (**File** menu, **Send E-mail** command), you can use the following keyboard shortcuts.

Important: Microsoft Office Outlook must be open before you can send e-mail messages. If Outlook isn't open, the message will be stored in your **Outbox** folder.

TASK	SHORTCUT
Send the current page or publication.	ALT+S
Open the Address Book when the cursor is in the e-mail message header.	CTRL+SHIFT+B
Open the Design Checker when the cursor is in the e-mail message header.	ALT+K

Check the names on the **To**, **Cc**, and **Bcc** lines against the Address Book when the cursor is in the e-mail message header.	CTRL+K
Open the Address Book with the **To** field selected when the cursor is in the e-mail message header.	ALT+. (period)
Open the Address Book with the **Cc** field selected when the cursor is in the e-mail message header.	ALT+C
Open the Address Book with the **Bcc** field selected when the cursor is in the e-mail message header and the **Bcc** field is visible. To display the **Bcc** field, when the **Mailing** toolbar is selected, press SHIFT+P, press the DOWN ARROW key to select **Bcc**, and then, and then press ENTER.	ALT+B
Go to the Subject field.	ALT+J
Open the Microsoft Office Outlook **Message Options** dialog box.	ALT+P
Open the **Custom** dialog box to create an e-mail message flag when the cursor is in the e-mail message header.	CTRL+SHIFT+G
Move the cursor to the next field in the e-mail message header when the cursor is in the e-mail message header.	TAB
Move the cursor to the previous field in the e-mail message header.	SHIFT+TAB

Alternate between the insertion point in the e-mail message header and the **Send** button in the Mailing toolbar.	CTRL+TAB
After you choose **Send as Message** (**File** menu, **Send E-mail** command), you can use the following keyboard shortcuts.	

After you choose or **Send Publication as Attachment** (**File** menu, **Send E-mail** command), you can use the following keyboard shortcuts.

TASK	SHORTCUT
Open the Address Book when the cursor is in the e-mail message header.	CTRL+SHIFT+B
Open the Address Book with the **To** field selected when the cursor is in the e-mail message header.	ALT+. (period)
Open the Address Book with the **Cc** field selected when the cursor is in the e-mail message header.	ALT+C
Open the Address Book with the **Bcc** field selected when the cursor is in the e-mail message header and the **Bcc** field is visible. This keyboard shortcut only works if there is a name in the **Bcc field**. To display the **Bcc** field, when the **Mailing** toolbar is selected, press SHIFT+P, press the DOWN ARROW key to select **Bcc**, and then, and then press ENTER.	ALT+B
Go to the Subject field.	ALT+J

Open the **Custom** dialog box to create an e-mail message flag when the cursor is in the e-mail message header.	CTRL+SHIFT+G
Move the cursor to the next field in the e-mail message header when the cursor is in the e-mail message header.	TAB
Move the cursor to the previous field in the e-mail message header.	SHIFT+TAB
After you choose **Send as Message** (**File** menu, **Send E-mail** command), you can use the following keyboard shortcuts.	

Automate Tasks.

Work with macros

TASK	SHORTCUT
Display the **Macros** dialog box.	ALT+F8

Work with Visual Basic

TASK	SHORTCUT
Display the Visual Basic editor.	ALT+F11

Customer's Page.

This page is for customers who enjoyed Office 2010 Keyboard Shortcuts For Windows.

Dearly beloved customer, please leave a review behind if you enjoyed this book or found it helpful. It will be highly appreciated, thank you.

Download Our Free EBooks Today.

In order to appreciate our customers, we have made some of our titles available at 0.00. Totally free. Feel free to get a copy of the free titles.

(A) For Keyboard Shortcuts In Windows

Go to Amazon: Windows 7 Keyboard shortcuts

Go to Other Stores: Windows 7 Keyboard Shortcuts

(B) For Keyboard Shortcuts In Office 2016

Go to Amazon: Word 2016 Keyboard Shortcuts For windows

Go to Other Stores: Word 2016 Keyboard Shortcuts For Windows

Note: Feel free to download them from your favorite store today. Thank you!

Other Books By This Publisher.

S/N	Title	Series
Series A: Limits Breaking Quotes.		
1	Discover Your Key Christian Quotes	Limits Breaking Quotes
Series B: Shortcut Matters.		
1	Windows 7 Shortcuts	Shortcut Matters
2	Windows 7 Shortcuts & Tips	Shortcut Matters
3	Windows 8.1 Shortcuts	Shortcut Matters
4	Windows 10 Shortcut Keys	Shortcut Matters
5	Microsoft Office 2007 Keyboard Shortcuts For Windows.	Shortcut Matters
6	Microsoft Office 2013 Shortcuts For Windows.	Shortcut Matters
7	Microsoft Office 2016 Shortcuts For Windows.	Shortcut Matters
8	Microsoft Office 365/2016 Keyboard Shortcuts For Macintosh.	Shortcut Matters
Series C: Teach Yourself.		
1	Teach Yourself Computer Fundamentals	Teach Yourself
Series D: For Painless Publishing		
1	Self-Publish it with CreateSpace.	For Painless Publishing
2	Where is my money? Now solved for Kindle and CreateSpace	For Painless Publishing
3	Describe it on Amazon	For Painless Publishing
4	How To Market That Book.	For Painless Publishing

CPSIA information can be obtained
at www.ICGtesting.com
Printed in the USA
BVHW01s1331160218
508355BV00013B/76/P